Seeds of Hope

The Life and Work of Patricia Brenninkmeyer

Leslie Read • Raymond Menino

First published in Great Britain in 2014 by Step Beach Press Ltd, Hove.

ISBN 978 1 908779 12 0

Typeset by Step Beach Press Ltd

Cover design by Steve Brenninkmeyer

Edited by Terry Philpot

Printed in Singapore by Star Standard Industries Pte Ltd

Step Beach Press Ltd, 28 Osborne Villas, Hove BN3 2RE
www.stepbeachpress.co.uk

Contents

Acknowledgements

We would like to thank the following individuals for the time they spent in talking to us about their memories of Patricia or support they gave us over the course of writing the book.

Kehinde Adeyemi, John Albert, Rosie Albert, David Barker, Gregory Brenninkmeyer, Michael Brenninkmeyer, Paul Brenninkmeyer, Thomas Brenninkmeyer, Madeleine Lustigman, Brian Evans, Sue Errington, Andrew Jones, Nightingale Kalinda, John Kasule, John Kennedy, Susan Kisitu, Heidi Kruitwagen, Elijah Kyamuwendo, Basil Kiwanuka, Sym Kiwanuka, Paulino Kiwanuka, Jane Leek, Grace Musoke, Peters Musoke, Beatrice Nabiteeko, the parents of Jessica Nakato, Elizabeth Namaganda, Julius Nkuraija, Val Ross, Rose Nasimiyu Rotuno, Father Sekalaga, Christine Semambo Sempebwa, Juliet Nakayiiwa, Anisha Rajapakse, Matilda Ssengooba, Canon Sentongo, Bishop Ssentongo, and Alastair Taylor. Terry Philpot read and edited the manuscript.

Leslie Read and Raymond Menino

1

Nothing is more practical than finding God,
that is, than falling in love in an absolute, final way.
What you are in love with,
what seizes your imagination,
will affect everything.
It will decide what will get you out of bed in the
mornings,
what you will do with your evenings,
how you spend your weekends,
what you read, who you know, what breaks your
heart,
and what amazes you with love and gratitude.
Fall in love, stay in love, and it will decide
everything.

Father Pedro Arrupe SJ

Foreword

Richard Dowden, director of the Royal African Society

I first met Patricia when I attended a preparation course before going to Uganda as a teacher in 1971. She was unassuming, spoke softly but with great conviction and authority. She was not a preacher but stressed above all the need to respect the people we would be trying to help and the culture in which we would be operating. As she spoke I began to realise that going to work in Africa was not about doing things to or for people who were worse off than us in Britain, but learning from them and accepting that they might be giving me more than I was giving them. Patricia knew that only through real partnerships of equality could her powerful leadership create something that would last and grow.

Patricia said she "felt uncomfortably well off". That is why she became a social worker. She sought the possibilities of equality and solidarity with the poor, an interaction with others that was not coloured by class division. Her wealthy, comfortable background, she said, "didn't matter one bit". This search for an egalitarian relationship with others went further than a professional career. It was her approach to life. She was one of the first social workers to recognise the need for cultural sensitivity in cases of the fostering of children from other parts of the world – something which is now universally accepted.

When a trainee social worker in Liverpool, she had learned that by listening to those with whom she worked – people who came from such a very different background from hers – she could bridge that distance. That was also her approach when she went to Uganda in 1964. Her mission, she said, was to understand "the real meaning of things, the customs and background". She spoke of her need to "absorb the culture and background" of Uganda.

That is what I learnt from her and what I tried, often ineptly and clumsily, to do when I went to Africa for two years. Later, as a journalist covering wars, upheavals and disasters – as well as ordinary life – throughout Africa, I tried always to get inside the culture and the minds of the people I met. I saw it as my mission to try to understand and explain why people did what they did, and accept and respect the validity of different cultures. I also tried to imagine what I would do if I woke up one morning and found myself unable to leave. If I had to stay there trapped in poverty and threatened by violence, crime or war, how long would I survive? These important lessons I learnt from Patricia's leadership.

I was also able to visit the Nsambya Babies Home where Patricia first worked on arrival in Uganda and which she supported long after leaving the country. It has provided abandoned children with a future and been an inspiration to generations of Ugandans.

As ever, long-sighted and sensitive, Patricia founded Kulika which addressed the problems of access to higher education for Ugandans and also trained subsistence farmers who lacked skills and capital, and later Ka Tutandike, for children of the poorest of the poor in market areas. In 2013 this organisation won the $10,000 prize in the annual international Project Inspire 'Inspirational Award' for a social enterprise initiative.

Patricia has changed the lives of many thousands of Ugandans in subtle but profound ways and influenced Uganda's national development. But she would be the last person to claim these achievements. She has always worked with others, engaged with them, inspired them and empowered them. Today she speaks of the "new partners to help carry the work into the future". They and their work will be her legacy.

Chapter I

The early years: Swimming against the tide

In late 1938, Patricia Brenninkmeyer, a babe in arms, moved from England, where she was born in Wimbledon earlier that year, with her family to their new home in Germany, in the industrial town of Essen, where they were to live for a year. It was during the first week there that her parents, Arnold and Catharina Brenninkmeyer, were to witness Kristallnacht, an orgy of destruction by Nazi hooligans, which saw the rounding up of Jewish families in the neighborhood in the middle of the night. Some were tied to trees while their homes and businesses were being wrecked. It was an event which took place throughout Germany but was only a portent of what was to come, symbolic of the world into which Patricia was born, as nations and ideologies raced towards collision. Fascist, anti-democratic regimes had arisen in Italy and Germany; General Franco had secured victory in Spain only months before; while

Communism had ruled in the Soviet Union for more than two decades.

Arnold and Catharina (always known as Toos, the Dutch diminutive of her Christian name) had been called to leave the relative stability of Britain and Wimbledon, where they had been settled for a decade, and the move to Germany was an effort to rejuvenate the leadership of the family business in that country in the face of the looming hostilities.

Such traumatic times, a world falling apart and soon to burst into flames, unleashing unprecedented horrors on vast populations, would have seemed inconceivable when Arnold was born on 21 October 1900, the fifth son and the eighth of 13 children of Clemens and Maria Augusta Brenninkmeyer, in the village of Mettingen, near Munster, Germany. He was the grandson of August Brenninkmeyer, one of the two founding brothers of what was to become the major European and now an inter-continental retail company, C & A. The family dates back hundreds of years, with most of its members in Arnold's generation still being born and bred in Mettingen. A feel for business, specifically retail, seems to be a part of the DNA of the Brenninkmeyers. Building on previously existing commercial links, the first C & A merchandise depot was opened in Sneek in 1841 in the Netherlands, from which the Brenninkmeyers traded, a five day walk from Mettingen.

Like his father and grandfather, after being educated in the local school, where he also played for the village football team, Arnold was sent for higher education to Paderborn and then to Munster. After school he joined the family business and in the course of time he would assist his colleagues in running the company. In 1922, he was one of the first three Brenninkmeyers to expand the company into the United Kingdom. With two very brief interludes in Holland and two in the north of England, he finally settled in London with responsibility for the stores in the UK.

Although, like Patricia, Arnold was basically a retiring person, uneasy in unfamiliar company, he was a consummate leader with clear vision and a strong work ethic. He was a reflective person, cared deeply about people, and was blessed with a great sense of humour and hearty laugh. All this was undergirded by an unquestioning loyalty to the Catholic Church, a profound faith and sense of personal prayer. Daily early morning mass before going to 'the Business' at 8am, and rosary with night prayers and the entire family on their knees after supper each evening – these were the bookends of his daily life. During the war the rosary was to become the family's prayer for peace.

Daily mass was voluntary for the family, but it was quite clear what the expectations were, and unless there was a real reason for not being there, all the children were on parade each morning with Arnold in the first contingent for the short trip to St Agatha's, the local parish church in Kingston. Early rising and punctuality for this parade were, however, not among Patricia's strong points. There was a big chauffeur-driven car – her father's poor eyesight precluded his ever driving for himself – but not all the children could fit in, so the younger ones, and Patricia, who was usually late, were expected to walk, whatever the weather, until the car, having delivered the first load at the church, would come back to pick up the walkers.

Though very glad to be living in Britain for the greater part of his life – it became his home from home – Arnold never became English in any sense of the word. He remained a foreigner there all his life, and liked it that way. Outside his warm relationships with his English business colleagues, his real social friendships, while significant, were few. He had no penchant for small talk.

While in many respects he was set in his ways, he was a man of enthusiasms, some of which – walking, reading, smoking cigars, gardening, being well informed and arguing his convictions with gusto – were long lasting, while others – smoking a pipe, photographing flora and fauna – he would try and then drop. Patricia inherited her love for nature and for gardening from her father, but expanded this into a great love for animals, especially for dogs. From her earliest years, she was drawn to care for them and was able to work with animals without any sense of fear.

In many ways Arnold was ahead of his time: in an age when to achieve an 'A' Level pass in secondary school was considered remarkable, it was typical of him to insist that both his daughters achieve not only 'A' Levels at school, but also receive an excellent university education. Patricia gained her university degree in geography at St Andrew's University followed by further qualifications in social work at Liverpool, while her older sister, Marylies, received her degree in psychology from the University of Nijmegen in Holland.

Later, after his retirement from day-to-day business life, Arnold embraced and gave new inspiration to the philanthropic activity of the family in England, working with top independent experts in the assessment, sponsoring and planning of projects in a way that was remarkable at that time. In later years, in her own philanthropic work, Patricia was to benefit greatly from the expertise and networking provided by the charitable organisation whose foundations were laid by her father.

Toos, born on 19 February 1901, was the youngest of three daughters of Cornelis van der Schoot, the owner of a wholesale iron company, specialising in, among other things, cast iron wood or coal fired heaters and ovens. This was in Tilburg, a sizeable provincial town in Brabant in southern Holland. Toos' mother, Elizabeth, née Wouters, also came from Brabant. Though Elizabeth's portrait featured prominently among the photographs on the family grand piano, she seemed to feature nowhere else. Toos rarely spoke about her mother, and little is known about her other than that she was the first woman to ride a bicycle in Tilburg, which for a woman, at least of her status at that time, was considered somewhat undignified. She died in 1918, when Toos was 17 years old. This left Cornelis to maintain a happy and united home for his three daughters, and to complete their education single handed. The two elder girls married and left home early to start their own families, but all three maintained a very warm and close relationship with each other and their father to his dying days.

Toos' family was also devoutly Catholic. Toos herself, while being a deeply spiritual person like Arnold, was not as wedded to all the externals of the exercise of her religion as he was. For her, prayer was not so much 'saying prayers'; her relationship with the Lord allowed her to chat with him in a personal, extemporaneous way.

Hers was a very practical spirituality. For Toos, going to Lourdes as matron of the train carrying sick and disabled people as part of the Dutch National Pilgrimage each year was a deep religious experience, to which she would often refer in later years. While she supported Arnold's routine for the family at daily night prayers, she was not so keen on the kneeling aspect of it, preferring to sit while everyone else was on their knees. This seeming casualness initially raised some eyebrows, although all could be explained by the realisation that she suffered from chronic rheumatism, and once on her knees, she was never quite sure how to get up again.

Her particular brand of spirituality would come out in refreshing *bon mots* to the children: "Reform the world – begin with yourself!"; "Courtesy is the custom of a king"; or "Our Lord is no policeman!" Patricia was later to sum up the situation succinctly: "Papa supplied the example of fervour while Mama brought things down to earth with her favourite sayings." When, on occasion, Arnold was not around in the evening, the rosary might be considerably delayed, or even forgotten altogether, while Toos held court at the supper table with lively discussions "often involving a lot of laughter in the family", says Patricia. This was another form of family spirituality.

After initial schooling in Tilburg, Toos was sent to a finishing school run by nuns. Here she came under the influence of the charismatic Soeur Marie, a French nun, whose wisdom and warmth, combined with her no-nonsense caring for her charges, left an indelible impression on Toos, and on many other young women, as they were about to be launched into life in the world outside provincial Brabant. When Cornelis retired from his day-to-day business life, he set about augmenting further his youngest daughter's education, as she accompanied him on travels to see the world. In the early 1920s this really only amounted to France, Italy and Switzerland for winter sports. The relationship between father and daughter remained special until he died in 1943. He spent many happy weeks and months visiting Toos and Arnold and their growing family in England.

Aenne Gockel, another young pupil from Soeur Marie's finishing school, was married to Arnold's eldest brother, Willy, another one of the three family members that founded the company in the United Kingdom. They lived in a house called 'Holmwood' on Kingston Hill outside London. It was a large house situated in its own gardens, a property that much later, after the Second World War, was to become the ultimate family home for Arnold and Toos and their children. However, in the 1920s Aenne's fond hope of many children to fill the house did not materialise. In Soeur Marie's view, she needed more support, a woman's intuition, and a friendly shoulder to lean on. Toos, her chosen means for this operation, was dispatched to Kingston for several months in 1927.

The 'Holmwood' garden included a tennis court, and while Toos was visiting, Arnold would come from London at weekends to play tennis. His poor eyesight was a bit of a handicap for him on the court, although he had a punishing serve. So long as he could intimidate his opponent with his customary barrage of aces he stood a fair chance of winning. Whilst he couldn't always connect with the ball on the court, he had no problem connecting with the young visitor from Tilburg. There is no record of Toos ever meeting her match on the court, but love was instantaneous, and marriage followed in Tilburg in 1929.

Toos was a challenging match as a life partner for Arnold. Although Arnold's enthusiastic love for Toos was perfectly clear to all, true to the conventions of the time, she seldom expressed her emotions in any public way. Her naturally outgoing spirit had been impeccably honed into the ways of a lady by Soeur Marie so that they became second nature to her and almost an art form: when sitting, she never used the back of her chair. Her ability in French, English and German, as well as her native Dutch, was an asset. Yet with all this grooming, she remained a fun-loving, enterprising young woman quite prepared to live her life according to her own lights, with an independence of spirit that was rare among 'ladies' in the society of the early 20th century.

No challenge was too great for her. Another piece of wisdom handed on to her children was that when faced with a choice between two good courses of action, one should always choose the more difficult or challenging one. Together with her immense self-control came an iron will and dauntless courage. She managed one day to give up chain smoking when she decided that her urge to smoke before breakfast was "disgusting!" She even learned to drive a car at the age of 50.

Patricia did not acquire these same qualities by chance. While Toos appreciated the social conventions of the time – which Patricia never did – neither was prepared to be ruled by them. Toos' father must clearly have encouraged this trait in her make up. Thus, in the days when it was not really done for young women to seek serious employment – and certainly not salaried employment – Toos chose to become qualified as a nurse, and worked successfully in that capacity for some years.

While Patricia showed many of the characteristics evident in her father, neither she nor her mother were able to recognise the strong character traits that they shared with each other. Neither could fully accept nor appreciate how very alike they were in their fundamental outlook and their giftedness. This partly explains the often faltering relationship between them, a hurdle that both regretted but neither knew how to overcome, while remaining their own person.

Toos was by nature vivacious, but not flamboyant. She was ever spontaneous and straight as a die in her outlook on life, as was Patricia. There were no airs and graces about either of them. Toos respected all people, regardless of their rank or station in life. What opinions or demands a bishop, mother superior or bemedaled military officer might or might not have would cut little ice with her because of who they were. With her Brabant warmth and charm, she would confront, often with remarkable personal courage, any who might walk over others, and in her pursuit of justice, or to safeguard those whom she considered to be getting a raw deal in life, she would tell them exactly what was what. At one stage, during the British occupation in Germany at the end of the War, an English officer demanded to know the whereabouts of a series of church banners that she had stowed away for safe-keeping. He wanted to use them to festoon an officers' garden party. Toos stood up to him, telling him that such a use would be utterly inappropriate. The officer, taken aback, said that if she would not comply, he would have to shoot her. "Go ahead", she retorted, "Shoot!". The more rigidly educated Arnold was on occasion embarrassed, not to say fearful of the consequences of her forthrightness, but could not help admiring his wife's single-minded, uncomplicated approach to all things.

Patricia, too, exhibited this same championing of the weak and vulnerable and, in her case, this was also extended, from an early age, to her fondness for and fascination with animals. In the 'Holmwood' garden squirrels were a continuing menace, so Arnold decided on setting traps to catch and dispose of them. These might well have effectively dealt with the problem were it not for the fact that Patricia went around after him to set all the squirrels free again. Such behavior was not at all appreciated – but the traps disappeared and were not seen again.

Frugality in day-to-day living was the goal. The children quickly learned the difference between 'needs' and 'wants', and although within that frugal framework they could be sure that what they needed would be supplied, they also learnt all about putting the needs of others first. The careful stewardship of all the gifts and benefits that came their way was instilled from the start. Quite deliberately, there was no pocket money for the children. All that they needed was provided, and if what was needed was money, a careful accounting for what was spent was expected – and any change returned.

The example of both parents of giving of themselves in a loving way, expressed very differently by each, and their striving for family unity at all costs, was the linchpin of their parenthood. It was truly their abiding gift to their children, and as they sincerely hoped, to their children's children also. This underpinned everything done in, or by the family.

In 1929 the newly married couple settled into their first home in Roehampton, a London suburb. Here the first two boys were born. It was quickly realised that, as a result of a medical misjudgment, John, the eldest, had contracted meningitis very shortly after his birth, which affected his cognitive capacity and his ability to speak. This tragedy would later be compounded by other serious physical disabilities. Years later, after the death of his parents, John was to play a significant part in Patricia's life when, for all practical purposes, she became his guardian. After the birth of Michael in 1932, the second of eight children, the young family moved to a larger home on Wimbledon Common. It was here that Toos gave birth to Derick in 1933, Marylies in 1934, Gregory in 1936, and eventually Patricia, the second daughter in the family, in 1938.

That year was also the year in which Arnold was requested to accept an unpopular assignment in Germany, but, true to form, he stoically relocated the family to their new home in the Alfredstrasse, in Essen. With its coal mines and steelworks, Essen was the centre of the industrial Ruhr district where Krupp was producing the weapons that were to keep the German war machine functioning. Therefore, when war came the area was exposed to continuous, severe air raids. In a place of so many factories the atmosphere had become so polluted with smog and floating soot that bringing up a family there was in itself a health hazard. So, after trying for a year to settle down, Arnold and Toos decided they had to find another solution, at least for the children.

Gregory, when still in England, had developed severe asthma and Michael was developing other health problems. For them an ideal solution was found: a children's health resort, run by a Dutch baroness in Oberstdorf, a small Bavarian mountain village, with a perfect climate and beautiful scenery – even if it was far away. The atmosphere and setting were so good that the remaining children were also sent there, leaving only baby Patricia with her mother.

Eventually, Arnold and Toos found a new family home in Mettingen, Arnold's birthplace, where his mother still lived. It belonged to cousins living in Holland, who also worked in the family business. They offered 'Marienhof', their summer house in Mettingen, to their cousin and his extensive family, for the remaining years of the War. This allowed them to bring their children back again under one roof, in the relative safety of the countryside, where – at least until the last few months of the war and subsequent unsettled period of the British occupation – local food was available to feed the growing family. Early in 1941 another son, Paul, was born, to be followed in 1943 by the arrival of Thomas, to complete the family.

Everyone soon settled down to life in war-time Mettingen. There were austerities to be coped with. That there was no hot water except on Saturday evenings was among the least of these. On that day enough water was heated in the kitchen and carried upstairs to fill a bathtub, and, in order of age, all the children were scrubbed down in quick succession. That was the beginning of the weekly celebration of

Sunday. Only one bomb – a stray landing in a field – fell to disturb the relative peace of Mettingen during the entire war, but there were regular air skirmishes above during which everyone knew their place in the shelter, and in the morning the children could pick up the spent bullet cases from the combats of the previous night.

All the older children, including Patricia, were enlisted in the village schools. From 1943 all teachers were gradually replaced with Nazi cronies, religion was banned from the school curriculum, and giving the Hitler salute was mandatory whenever passing a civil servant, teacher, town mayor and other dignitaries, although the children had no real understanding of what it all meant. In the days before television, the children, together with their school mates, learned to entertain themselves and play in very imaginative ways. It was safe for the whole village to be their playground, and the older ones made good use of it. From a child's perspective it seemed like a paradise – almost unreal even as war raged all around.

Arnold was the only one to experience what was going on outside this little 'paradise' for he was still responsible for the business in the Ruhr district and had to be on the road all week every week to keep the business going, and was home only at the weekends. Meanwhile in Mettingen, the gardens were ploughed up to grow potatoes, carrots, spinach, and rhubarb. Pigs were kept surreptitiously, and from time to time one would be butchered at night behind locked doors by the village women, including Toos, and turned into cuts of meat and sausages. That such activity was forbidden by the regime was no deterrent. While Patricia was too young to have any notion of what war was all about, the combination of all that was going on around her must have had a significant impact on her.

Patricia and Gregory formed a special bond that remains to this day. Both had the same adventuresome streak in their makeup. She reflected later: "We were in the middle of the family, too young to be allowed to join the activities of the older ones, and definitely too big to be included with the little ones. Yet we made our presence felt and gave Arnold and Toos more headaches than all the others put together!"

Gregory and Patricia, partners in crime that they were, the ones most consistently in trouble, most often bore the brunt of their mother's displeasure. They just did not know how not to be naughty, to the extent that, whenever there was a lull in family life, with not much of note going on, it was assumed that Gregory, and especially Patricia, must be up to no good. Their mother was blessed with penetrating dark brown eyes. She could make her eyes dance with fun and pleasure, but by the same token, she effectively controlled the entire family with them, often without a word being said.

But there were also some issues between sister and brother. Patricia told Gregory: "You made friends easily and were never far from trouble. Incidentally, when you and Marylies played 'Father and Mother' I resented always having to be 'the child' together with the dolls!" Patricia never had any time for dolls, so this must have been particularly galling.

At the end of hostilities came peace and the Allied occupation. Because of the size of the house and its proximity to the main road through the village, 'Marienhof' caught the eyes of the occupying forces, who commandeered it. The family had 24 hours' notice which allowed them no time to take most of their belongings with them. They found an enlarged cottage, the home of the local dentist, the most prominent Nazi of the village, who had been taken to a camp for political prisoners. This new home was so small that, at least, it would not attract the eye of the occupying forces.

These were really unsettling times for Arnold and Toos. The fact that their Dutch passports and other identification papers had previously been confiscated added to their frustration. Consequently, without proof to the contrary, they were assumed to be the enemy by the British and treated with scant respect. Looting by the occupying forces was the order of the day, much of the property was destroyed and personal belongings and furniture disappeared. In later years, in Bournemouth in England, Toos was aghast to find a local woman wearing one of her dresses that had been specially designed for her and which she had last seen in 'Marienhof'!

Once settled into their cottage, the time came for Patricia to make her first Holy Communion. Somehow she was dressed in a white dress and veil and driven to church in a horse-drawn carriage belonging to her grandmother – there was no petrol for the few cars then available – and afterwards there was a great celebratory meal for the family and various guests in an upper room – the boys' bedroom. For Toos nothing was impossible and here again she pulled off a real *tour de force*.

Patricia was later to reflect on those war-time years: "Early school years in Mettingen were, in fact, very colourful and great fun, just tinged with enough excitement and shortages without being very dangerous in the eyes of us children. But how much they have affected the way we have come to see life in later years!"

On 3 February 1946 the time came for Patricia's elder siblings to move to Holland, to learn the language and go on to boarding school. They all departed, together with assorted cousins, in an army truck one morning, causing further anguish in the family. The departure of Gregory, somewhat later and by himself, was particularly upsetting for her. It was hard being suddenly bereft of her closest friend and ally in a tough world. In her own words Patricia says she was "devastated!" Aged eight and a half, she was now left to get on with her two younger brothers, aged six and four, as best she could. They were no substitute for Gregory and no one could say when she would see the others again.

On 20 April 1947 the day dawned that Arnold and Toos, together with their three youngest children, were able to make the journey out of Germany into freedom, as Arnold had been assigned to supervise the stores in Holland. However, before they could go, they had to undergo the tiresome but compulsory repatriation procedure in order to receive new travel documents. Time was needed to prepare their new home and so, as a temporary measure, the family stayed in a hotel in Hilversum in Holland. The relief was such that in a very rare display of emotion, Toos burst into tears – tears of joy, tears of bewilderment – at all that the family's new life promised, and tears, too, at seeing clothes in the shops, and also oranges and bananas and bacon once more for sale, none of which the children had ever seen before.

In a country that hated all things German, Arnold and Toos let it be known that the family had recently migrated from Switzerland to make a new life in Holland. The latter part of that statement was true and sufficed until Paul, in his innocence, let the side down. In his enthusiasm, having the time of his life riding on a tram packed with people – another new adventure – he shouted out at the top of his voice: "Heil Hitler!" with the appropriate salute, to the consternation of all around him. In the resulting uproar, the family was summarily turned off the tram to continue on foot.

Toos arranged for the English nanny, who had taken care of all the older children in Wimbledon in the pre-war years, to come to Holland to knock some civilised behavior into the three village bumpkins from the backwoods of Germany. Nanny was on a losing wicket: she spoke only English and the children only German, and with Patricia in the forefront, the three of them led her a merry dance in the busy streets of Hilversum where the family now lived, until disaster struck. At a children's party in the hotel where they were staying, Tom fell through an upstairs plate glass window, landing on his head in front of the hotel receptionist's desk. He sustained a fractured skull and was taken to hospital in a critical condition – another separation for Patricia. Would he survive? When would she see him again? These fearful thoughts would easily fill the imagination of a little girl in these uncertain circumstances.

Then the family business career took yet another unexpected turn as Arnold was sent to spearhead the rebuilding of the company in England. However, with Tom in hospital, Arnold and Toos could not leave Holland. It was decided that Patricia and Paul would travel to England in the early autumn of 1947 with Nanny and live in a hotel in Ascot until such a time as Tom was well enough to travel, and then at least the younger members of the family could be reunited.

Poor Nanny had a terrible time of it as Patricia and Paul ran rings around her, and being complete strangers in the world of dowagers, crumpets, and cucumber sandwiches, were mischievous and playful with things they did know about. Then, not before time, law and order was restored, as Arnold and Toos, with Tom in tow, arrived back in England and took control once more.

A house was found – again on Wimbledon Common – too small, but a palace compared to what they had lived in since they had last lived in England. This was temporary accommodation until, by chance, 'Holmwood' on Kingston Hill, which had been owned by Willy and Aenne before the War, came on the market and was snatched up by Arnold and Toos. And so the place where, years ago, they had met for the first time, became their family home for the next 34 years.

Toos was delighted to be back on familiar territory and busied herself putting the household together again. It was so good to be warmly welcomed back by local shop assistants and others whom she had known just before the War. It was like coming home again; all the experiences of the past years in Germany felt like a bad dream, but they, too, were now gradually fading away.

There remained the problem of what to do about the education of the two daughters. The choice fell on the Convent of the Sacred Heart in Woldingham, Surrey, a highly esteemed girls' boarding school run at the time by the Sisters of the Sacred Heart. But it was already September, and the school term was due to start at the end of that month. Unperturbed, Toos contacted the headmistress, the formidable Mother Shanley, to explain her dilemma, and to ask if room could be found at the eleventh hour for Marylies and Patricia. When Mother refused the request saying: "I simply don't have the beds", Toos retorted: "But I can provide those".

Marylies and Patricia joined the school at the end of the month and Toos and Mother Shanley developed a great respect for each other over the years. As it turned out, both girls were assets to the school. Both displayed gifts of leadership and received the much-coveted Blue Ribbon when they reached the upper sixth form – and by dint of hard work, on the part of both the girls and their teachers, each gained more than one of those prestigious 'A' Levels.

The transition from village life in post-war Germany to academic life in the strange environment of an English boarding school, on top of learning a new language, proved tough for Patricia. Study did not come naturally to her, nor was it to her taste. She much preferred the rough and tumble of outdoor life, climbing trees and communing with various forms of wildlife to the business of learning and classroom discipline. She fell out of a tree one day and broke her arm – after that life changed and she had to take her studies more seriously.

Patricia's account of her academic achievements is characteristically both humble and humorous. She remembered: "My academic achievements at school are best glossed over swiftly. Let us say that results were laboriously attained, and that most of the effort was put in by my parents, and that all too often things came to roost in the holidays." Then extra tuition and further study were arranged if any lack of the desired progress was detected. Always an avid reader, she eventually became a hard-working student, and also learned to express herself creatively in writing. She chose geography for her 'A' Level specialty, along with German. The young Mother Bell had her as her first ever 'A' Level student and as such, their joint enterprise was quite an achievement. Patricia developed a real love for the subject, which eventually led to her university degree at St Andrews.

Quite apart from academic life, for Patricia the school strongly underscored the same ideals and principles of life, the promotion of social awareness and the importance of her Catholic faith, that had been instilled into her at home.

There were, of course, any number of archaic expectations in daily convent school life. All pupils were required to curtsey in front of the portrait of Mother Foundress that hung halfway up the grand stairway in the main building; a hazardous performance as the students stampeded down to the dining hall below. The food left a good deal to be desired: Patricia once discovered a dishcloth stewing in a teapot provided for their morning refreshment. Yet, despite the discipline of the strict regime, Patricia grew to enjoy school life and all it had to offer. Some of her fellow pupils became life-long friends.

One such friend was Anne, eldest daughter of the Duke and Duchess of Norfolk. In one school holiday Patricia was invited to the family home at Arundel Castle for a long weekend as the guest of her school friend. Both Arnold and Toos had major misgivings about this: she would feel out of place among the lords and ladies that were presumed to be there. Would she make some awful social *faux pas* and disgrace herself, or would she suddenly become very homesick? Despite these doubts, on the appointed day, Patricia was put on the train to Arundel with her suitcase containing clothes for every possible eventuality, including riding gear for the fox hunt, which was to be the highlight of the weekend's entertainment.

The Duke, Duchess and Anne were delighted to see her when she arrived, and could not have been more hospitable. The great day of the hunt dawned. An impressive hunting party had assembled, all decked out in their white riding jodhpurs and pink jackets. The horses and the hounds were at the ready. Patricia, with her riding gear and hat, was also ready and looked the part. She was given a quiet mount, but was clearly feeling out of place as her mother had predicted. Her nervousness must have communicated itself to her pony which, even before the hunt had got properly underway, stalled at some hazard and sent Patricia flying into the mud. That was the end of her hunting experience – and probably not to Patricia's dismay. She did not approve of hunting and killing animals. And all the concern at home about her going at all was enough to make even the boldest young girl nervous. The relief on all sides at her safe, albeit early return from Arundel was palpable. This foray into the social high life revealed a need for a little more practice.

Patricia's later reflections on her childhood and upbringing, and her relationships with the wider family, largely living in Holland, are particularly revealing. She wrote: "We do have a great deal in common: our family, our religion, our prosperity and our almost unique upbringing in a harmonious home... some of the things which I kicked against, which (at the time) niggled and worried me."

In another letter she mused on the importance of the tumultuous war years and their aftermath, making the point that she could stand firm in the face of adversity because of the strength of the family:

> Perhaps because of our unsettled childhood our family liked to be on the move. This brings an amazingly international perspective to every kind of discussion in the family. In spite of our extraordinarily different lifestyles and national flavours, we're an extremely close family unit, and we work at keeping it that way, because we each gain a great deal of strength and confidence from each other in an otherwise difficult and confusingly angry world.

The Sacred Heart nuns had done their best to turn Patricia into a young lady, with moderate success. However, Toos was not about to give up on turning Patricia into the daughter she believed Arnold wanted her to be. Whether she was right in this surmise or she was motivated by her own values is open to debate, but she was determined. An insight into her dreams for Patricia came to light when, at about this time, an eminent photographer in London was invited to make studies of both Marylies and Patricia. Both were in full evening dress for the occasion, and both had had their hair styled before this important appointment. Marylies' portraits were predictably beautiful and true to form. Patricia, on the other hand, with her hair frizzed up in permanent waves, came out of the session looking too angelic, just like a doll that she so hated; perhaps like her parents might have wanted her to be, but not at all like Patricia. Her portrait was mercifully soon forgotten. Nor was it replaced until very much later on.

When at home on holidays from school, Patricia's close family life clicked back into place. Boarding school and the long separation from home life meant that the holidays could be savoured all the more. Patricia says that holidays at 'Holmwood' were fun, a time to get "deeply involved in war games with lead soldiers in the attic interspersed with ping-pong". The home, according to Tom, was "big but cosy"; the family could all "fit in together because we belong together". Certainly, he goes on to reflect, there were "some friends more suitable for the pub and other friends suitable for the home". While the children were still very young, they tended to follow their own routines in the nursery. However, once they reached the magic age of 12, they were gradually allowed to join visits to the theatre, operas and musicals. Patricia took great pleasure in these cultural trips and speaks of the convoluted, romantic German librettos, when Gregory would read her the background stories of these operas. She relished the fact that he could sing "all those operatic arias which stirred our hearts".

With their father, the elder children enjoyed a warm and close relationship, endless conversations, deep discussions, and enjoyed regular evening games of either bridge or canasta.

Patricia mixed these genteel activities with playful pranks. Her brothers recount a game of hide-and-seek when she made off in the back of a car with a contingent of her elder siblings, leaving her younger brothers to hunt for her in vain around the garden at 'Holmwood' till darkness made any further hunt impossible. At that stage she returned, all smiles, having had a wonderful outing.

She would read stories to her younger brothers and was "good fun", according to Tom, but he also speaks from experience about "the strong right arm of a strong-willed older sister". Paul adds that "Patricia did not suffer fools gladly". Yet her humorous, playful and often mischievous character always shone through as a great strength.

The periods between terms at the Sacred Heart were also occasions for family travels around Europe. Patricia recounts "those wonderful summer holidays with all the family, climbing mountains, swimming and acting posh in those dreadful smart hotels". Most family holidays involved walking and enjoying nature. There were treks through the Black Forest and over the Dolomite mountains, the Bavarian Alps and the Scottish Highlands.

Patricia remembers the tremendous repertoire of songs, ranging from pieces from German operettas, through music hall songs to the latest English pop songs. With the family limousine at the ready, Arnold and Mr Boreham, the chauffeur, sat in the front and Toos sat in the rear, and children piled in as best they could. Another car would follow to bring the luggage and the overflow of youngsters, and so began the drive across Europe. The list of songs grew with the years and became ever more varied. Arnold had a resonant singing voice normally only heard in church, but, by way of exception, also on these trips. In Patricia's words: "We could fill that great car with music from London to Bavaria with no problem at all."

Despite this all-pervasive emphasis on togetherness each of the children was able to play their own distinctive part in the evolution of family values and their expression as they negotiated their way through the world of the late 1950s and 60s that was undergoing a wealth of cultural renewal. Derick was the first to strike out in new directions, bringing jazz into the home, to supplement the preferred classical music, and wearing jeans which his father thought vulgar and, according to Tom, "on the road to becoming a hippie!".

During the 1950s, Michael joined the Jesuits, eventually being sent to support the Christian community in Homs in Syria. Gregory and Paul would follow him into the priesthood in due course. True to the traditions of their various orders they all vowed to embrace the simple way of life within their communities. Patricia, too, like her brothers who joined the clergy, felt the urge to make a radical contribution to establish a more equitable and holistic society. Politics was not an avenue that interested her. As Gregory said, looking back at her life: "She's apolitical. She doesn't read the paper in England and she didn't read the paper in Uganda. It gave her an unpretentious outlook on life." Nor was her religion to be the overt channel for her energies: she had a very simple but very practical faith and prayer life expressed in doing the right thing for people in most need. She was interested in, and was moved by, the lives of those people she met and with whom she interacted. In Africa she found her inspiration, and this would become a deciding factor in shaping her life.

The call of Africa surfaced very early in Patricia's life – even when she was an eight year-old in Mettingen. She recounted later:

> I was sent to the Agatha Schule, and there, among other things, I was given piano lessons. Neither this nor any subsequent teacher ever taught me to play even the simplest tune on the piano, but this teacher could be diverted from the task by being encouraged to tell me stories about the little black children in Africa. She so fired my imagination that from then on, I was determined to go to Africa myself. All through my childhood I loved books on wild animals. As I grew up, I read all I could about lions and zoos and things which I felt would be useful to know about. In fact, my family has always known that I

was going to Africa. Just what I would do when I got there was less clear.

One expression of the hospitality of Arnold and Toos took the form of regular Sunday evening dinners to which a Dutch missionary priest friend, Father (later Bishop) Jan De Reeper from the Mill Hill Missionary Society, would be invited. He would regale Patricia and all at the dinner table with exciting and often deeply moving stories about his experiences in the African missions. He exercised a formative influence on her as she became more and more interested in missionaries' and explorers' tales.

Patricia's parents were "mildly alarmed" at the development of their daughter's interests. However, she would not give up on what they thought was a childish obsession with Africa, and so they struck a deal with her.

At the time, all entrants to St Andrew's University were required to have an 'A' Level in Latin, whatever subject they were hoping to read. Patricia's 'A' Levels were in geography and German. So Latin would need to be added after school by means of private tuition at home. Patricia and Latin did not get on at all, and the 'A' Level in Latin remained an intractable problem for her. Arnold and Toos proposed, therefore, that they would take Patricia to Africa together with Father de Reeper, the deal being that he and she would study Latin every morning, leaving the afternoons free for him to show Patricia and her parents the realities of life in that continent. She explained: "When I left school, my parents took me on a trip to South Africa, partly to confront me with the reality of Africa, and hoping to put me off it. I was a very contrary teenager!"

The deal did not work out: it did nothing for her mastery of Latin and only increased her desire for Africa. It was a trip that struck her forcefully in a new and meaningful way as she was confronted with severe racial injustice. She recalled: "Apart from being frightfully nice to all the poor, down-trodden black people, and being very incensed at the injustices I could see all around me, I was totally unqualified to do anything much to help them."

Her path was chosen, yet she faced a dilemma. In a letter she wrote years later, she looked back and expressed it as follows:

> I was upset by the Apartheid problems [in South Africa] and by the contrast of the rich hotels, in which we lived, and the beggars at the hotel entrances – and the poverty of the Africans. My imagination was working overtime, and I had great plans worked out for giving my parents the slip and staying behind, and doing my bit there and then to sort things out in South Africa! Well, of course I had never made any real decisions for myself and was far too much of a coward to do anything so brazen. But the trip certainly didn't put me off the idea of going to work in Africa.

So for Patricia it was back to the reality and to her Latin studies at home in Kingston. However, to add variety and spice to her existence, it was decided that she would also benefit from a spell at the Lucy Clayton School of Charm, then well known in London. Patricia dutifully went each morning and came home in the afternoon to regale everyone at the dinner table with stories and practical demonstrations of what she had learned: how to get into the back seat of a car backwards as a lady should, and what to do with her handbag and gloves, and that to wear one's jewelry before midday was vulgar. This experiment did not last long as even her mother could see that it was getting nowhere in producing the desired effect of turning out a proper lady.

Having eventually achieved her 'A' Level in Latin, it was arranged that Patricia should attend a finishing school course in Rome and Perugia, Italy, living with the Grail Society (usually known as The Grail), a religious group of lay women known to Arnold and Toos. The Italian sojourn proved to be a success. Patricia was happy with her exposure to all the cultural and artistic wonders that that country offers, and with her new-found relative freedom away from home and its expectations.

Patricia's artistic sensitivity in terms of fabric and colour co-ordination was expressed in her own free-spirited way; she loved arranging flowers and was good at it, but would invariably choose more unconventional wild flowers for her creations.

But Patricia's choices and character were always judged against those of her older sister, Marylies, who appeared to be the exact opposite of her in her outlook and bearing. Marylies was always proper, always punctual, always helpful and caring, well turned out for every occasion, always neat and tidy. She was also a diligent student, which was a constant struggle for Patricia. Marylies was, in fact, the model daughter, and her parents could only dream and pray that Patricia would turn out likewise.

However, Patricia's gifts were to emerge very differently. Yet in her untidy, erratic, idiosyncratic ways, with all her outdoor interests, she was forever being faced with this paragon of virtue whom she had no inclination or, indeed, ability to emulate. The girls shared a bedroom where a strict delineation of turf was established – the neat and tidy half was Marylies' domain, and the rest, a mess, belonged to Patricia. They had to share the writing desk which was somewhat problematic. And while they cared about each other deeply, the scenes in the bedroom were often less than cordial, as Patricia worked out her frustrations on her older sister in less than lady-like fashion.

Like her mother, Patricia was a free spirit, both strong willed and determined, and in many ways fearless, too. From a very early age she found the conventions of the times, particularly as presented in her home, unnecessary and irksome. In her effort to express herself and to give vent to the issues about which she cared most deeply, she manifested a formidable, crusading spirit. She seemed determined to rattle the cages of the more conventional members of the family, beginning with her mother, and others outside it, by the things she did deliberately to startle and shock them into new ways of thinking and seeing, and accepting the world around them as she herself saw it. Such behavior was not calculated to endear her to those who loved her most, or to promote their understanding of the issues involved. Only slowly did Patricia learn to challenge in a non-confrontational way.

Toos' real effort to understand her unruly daughter, and to do what was best for her wellbeing, was often blocked by the fact that they shared so many of the same instincts and concerns – instincts her mother, with her iron self-discipline, and the backing of the conventions of the time, had harnessed into a force for good within the context and expectations of the society of the 1920s. Patricia grew up in a time when the world was changing radically: old nostrums were being challenged, authority was being questioned, 'flower power' was rife, freedom of expression was exalted, and there was a growing human rights movement concerned with social equality.

All these developments painted a very different picture of a world she saw as difficult and confusing and where there was anger, and which called for very different responses. For her, many of the social and even spiritual values to which she was being asked to conform in those early days were debatable. Patricia found it hard to swallow them all as self-evident truths. She did not believe in all the certainties of the past that seemed to dictate the way the future should be, and at the time there were few with whom she could dare to debate these issues without immediately being put right by someone in authority.

Patricia's wonderful gift of accepting and quietly relating to people of vastly different backgrounds and abilities, drawing them together to co-operate in common enterprise, is the hallmark of her achievements both in England and later in Uganda. In the struggles and formative experiences of her early life, in her interaction with so many different and often strong personalities along the way, we find the seedbed that gave shape to a life of remarkable dedication to the wellbeing of thousands who are the richer for having known her and benefitted from her work.

Chapter II

Look through any window:
Life as a social worker

Perched on a windowsill in Perugia, the prospect of Umbria before her, Patricia plotted the course of her life during her 19th summer. Within the framed idyll she sat "for hours, watching the swallows" and contemplating. The hills and valleys, punctuated by medieval church towers and Roman aqueducts under an azure sky, might conceivably have had a strong influence on the direction of thought. A life in an area like this was more than feasible. Patricia had after all been sent off to Italy to be 'finished' after five years walking through the 700 acre estate and Victorian halls of her boarding school in Woldingham in Surrey. A decision surfaced: "It was here that I decided that social work was to be my life."

The decision in Perugia took her first, in 1961, to the neglected inner-city terraces of Liverpool – areas which later in that decade would be re-designated as slums and demolished. The view from her window in

Perugia could not have looked more different than the environment that she now encountered – the two images make an unlikely diptych – but Patricia was sure that she had chosen the correct path. Before Liverpool, she wrote to one of her mother's friends who ran a children's home in Belgium and requested a month's work experience to get a feel for the vocation. She sought to find out whether she wanted to do residential social work which would involve immersion in a children's home. She found work in the field to be her ideal vocation. The seeds of her passion for work in children's homes in England and Uganda were sown.

So strong was her desire to become a social worker that she wanted to skip the undergraduate arts degree at St. Andrew's that her parents wished her to pursue. It struck her as "a complete waste of time" especially considering that she could do her social work training without first gaining an undergraduate qualification. Most social workers were not graduates during the 1960s and 1970s. Indeed, it was to be more than ten years before some social services departments could boast having 100 per cent qualified workforces.

The tendrils of Patricia's parents continued to hold her however, and she had to consider their reasons for wishing her to complete a degree at St. Andrew's. Her discussion with friends led her to think, after all, that "a degree would be useful" and the conflict of wishes – of Patricia's to plunge straight into social work and her parents' that she should consider a more conventional arts degree – was resolved. She went to

St. Andrew's quite willingly and had what she describes as a "very happy time", putting off her social work training for four years. During this time she still harboured and nurtured her "ultimate aim" – to train as a social worker.

Having achieved her degree and with her parents temporarily pacified, Patricia started the two-year Diploma in Applied Social Studies at Liverpool University in 1961. This course – combining the theoretical and the practical – led Patricia to placements in the poorest areas of Liverpool. The first jarring challenge occurred during her time there. She swiftly found that the lives of those that she had to assist were completely different from her own. Colleagues would remind her that she had no idea what living a life of poverty entailed. For all her feelings about being "uncomfortably well off", the issues encountered by the victims of domestic abuse, for example, stood a great distance from her own life experiences. She describes the situation best herself: "I had loads of sympathy for people and plenty of common sense backed up by good training, but, boy, did I lack experience." Her passion for social work still burnt but there was also a daunting realisation that she had chosen an incredibly taxing path.

This became apparent during one of her earliest cases in Liverpool, which inducted her into the social worker's world of encountering innumerable intimate personal struggles. An affable and compassionate young woman in her early 20s, she was welcomed by a middle-aged Liverpudlian woman who promptly served her with "the usual slopped cup of tea". While the two of them drank the tea, the woman divulged her horrific story. Left at home by her husband every night she would wait with the agonising knowledge that, after closing time, her heavily drunken spouse would eventually stumble in her direction. Such was his inebriation that he would need her assistance simply in order to get into bed. Once there, he would soak both himself and his wife with urine as he could muster neither the strength nor ability to get up and use the toilet.

The true nature of the difficulties of field work made their keen impact felt. Patricia's justifiable dismay came not just from the visceral reaction to her first glance through the window of a despondent life. What also troubled her was the extreme distance between this tale told by the woman in front of her and what she had experienced in her own life. She felt inadequate; calling herself "little me", she could not understand why this woman was confiding in her. She worried that there was very little that she could actively do in order to improve this woman's life. However, it soon became apparent that, simply by sharing her problems with Patricia, the woman was able to purge herself of some of her anger and sadness. Patricia's lack of personal knowledge about the woes of an impoverished life, bereft of not only money but love and respect, was of no consequence as long as she was there to be confided in. She was buoyed by this discovery and aimed to improve her confidence in addition to researching and endeavouring to gain as much relevant experience as possible.

While taking her course, Patricia managed to get a practical work placement with immigrants in London in 1962, which she judged to be a valuable experience for future social work. Here she worked largely with West Indian immigrants who had not long arrived in the country. Attitudes towards these families held by many British people stood in stark contrast to their hospitality and kindness toward her. The Notting Hill Race Riots of 1958 had marked an explosion of racial tension. Senior police officers ignored their constables' reports on the 400 white people attacking the homes of West Indians on Bramley Road in Notting Hill, leading to violent interchanges for eight nights. They reported to the Home Secretary, R.A. Butler, that there was barely any racial motivation behind the tumultuous events, even if in reality the underlying problems of racism and discrimination were, indeed, there.

In 1959, three years prior to Patricia's arrival in London, Oswald Mosley was able to take a break from his eight year Parisian exile and attempt to win a seat at Kensington North during the General Election. Such was the atmosphere regarding immigration that his indecorous and criminal escapades leading the Blackshirts decades before were overlooked as the leader of pre-war British fascism was allowed to run for office as leader of the Union Movement. He was defeated but in April 1962, the year of Patricia's arrival in London, Parliament passed the Commonwealth Immigration Act which restricted the entry of immigrants (but particularly those who were black and Asian) to Britain.

There were various racist organisations formed to
combat what they saw as the threat from immigration
from the black Commonwealth. Some of these merged,
some became extinct, and some, to an extent,
prospered, like (for a while) the White Defence League
and, later, the British National Party, the National
Socialist Movement and the British Movement. All led
with the cry, "Keep Britain White", stirring up much
ill-feeling and racism, to make even tentative steps
toward doing away with discrimination difficult.
Alongside this kind of political agitation and the
breaking out of civil disturbances, immigrants had to
suffer everyday discrimination. It was, for example,
not illegal at this time to be refused entry to public
houses and other public places, to be refused jobs, or
to be denied housing on the basis of race or colour.

In addition to the constant racism encountered by the
West Indian families that Patricia worked with, they
were pushed into a life of poverty. Once posts in
public institutions such as British Rail and the
National Health Service had been filled, private
employment was difficult to attain as the employers
had free reign to deny positions because of their
prejudiced views of black people. Even trade unions
often denied help to African-Caribbean workers. All
this meant that the sharp suits and dual-coloured
brogues of those descending the gangplanks of
incoming ships, worn for the journey of hope to an
England deemed the 'mother country', would be
packed away as interview after interview all too often
ended negatively. For housing, too, interviews often

led to disappointment, as satirised at the time by Nobel Laureate Wole Soyinka when the 'Telephone Conversation' of his poem's title ends with a white potential landlady slamming her phone receiver down after asking such demeaning questions as "How dark?"

Patricia was shocked by what she deemed the appalling housing conditions and poverty experienced by the West Indians that she worked with in 1962. She held great affection for the families that she encountered and her period in London helped her to appreciate that there was fundamentally no difference between people of other races and herself. This in spite of living in a country riddled with racism, where friction between black and white was overt and violent as well as deeply ingrained within the minds of millions of inhabitants, and stoked by the right wing media. From close and touchingly intimate contact with West Indians living in London, Patricia concluded "that they were just ordinary people like me". After working with children whom she visited at home, she was further convinced that social work with children was the ideal calling for her.

Chapter III

And so to Africa

Patricia's heart always lay in Africa. The continent had captivated her since those early, magical stories during her childhood piano lessons, nourished by Father De Reeper's dinner time accounts of his mission at Kisumu in Kenya. To her young self, De Reeper's stories evoked an Africa, as Patricia saw it, which was full of adventure and danger, dense, primordial tropical forests and sun-bleached savannah, the home of tribes that lived by rules entirely alien to her civilised home. It was also a place without roads, hospitals or proper care services, where disease was rife, and where only very few people had any education. To her parents, it was certainly not the place where she would meet a prospective husband. Yet Patricia pressed on with her dreams of Africa and, after several dinners with De Reeper at their home, 'Holmwood', where the priest reassured her worried parents, there came an ideal opportunity.

And now, after a lifetime of telling everyone that she was going to work in Africa, she "couldn't possibly back out". One evening at 'Holmwood' in late 1963, the family entertained a dinnertime guest and friend of De Reeper's, Dr Magdalena Oberhofer, who had recently returned from a small country right at the heart of Africa, where the Nile began its journey to the Mediterranean: Uganda. Oberhofer had been working with The Grail, the lay women's international organisation, which was already known to Patricia through her time in Italy. The Grail, which is now ecumenical, was made up of young women from Holland, England and Germany trained in social work or healthcare and eager to make a difference in the world. In 1953 the sisters (as Grail members are known) established themselves in Uganda and occupied a small site right at the centre of Ugandan Catholicism's administrative headquarters on Rubaga Hill in Kampala. This hill site, just south of the centre of Kampala, commanded a view of Kampala's lush tropical hills and was where the White Fathers, French Catholic missionaries, had set up their first mission in the country in the 1870s. The Grail's compound was shared with Rubaga Hospital, where a cluster of European expatriate nurses, doctors and social workers were based.

It was during this meeting with Madgalena that everything fell into place. Patricia did not join The Grail, yet it was through them that she was able to get a foot into Africa, and early in 1964, the 25 year-old, air ticket in hand, left her London apartment to start her life 4,000 miles to the south, in a country that straddled the Equator.

Patricia recalled:

> I arrived at 6a.m. in Kampala. It was
> pouring and there was no one to meet me.
> The telegram I had sent to alert Rubaga of
> the change of flight reached them three
> days later! I was very tired. I had no idea if
> the telephone had been discovered in
> Uganda and whether Rubaga had a
> number. A very nice customs official took
> me in hand and an hour later I was fetched
> and on my way to Kampala. Here I was
> further disappointed because Rubaga
> wasn't primitive at all. It is situated on top
> of a hill with the best view of Kampala and
> miles around. I was given a little room of
> my own and advised to have a refreshing
> bath with hot water coming out of the taps
> like anywhere else. It all looked very
> European in paradise surroundings.
> A good sleep got things a little more into
> perspective.

Patricia's arrival came only two years after the country
had been granted independence from Britain. That
year, the first post-independence election had been
won by an alliance of the Uganda People's Congress
and Kabaka Yekka and saw Milton Obote installed as
executive prime minister, with the Kabaka (king) of
Buganda, Edward Muteesa II, holding the largely
ceremonial role as president.

But of more immediate importance to Patricia was that at The Grail's Rubaga Hospital compound she first met a young Ugandan woman in her early 20s who was training to be a social worker. Elizabeth Namaganda wore a stern face that carried an authority and determination which had been vital to her progress through secondary and higher education, yet her wide smile would often break out, putting those that surrounded her at ease. Elizabeth would become one of Patricia's life-long friends and would later become one of the first African women to join The Grail, eventually leading their Ugandan community. "Yet at the time, as a young woman studying", Elizabeth reflected, "I felt interacting with these white people whom everyone admires was something very exciting".

It was not the status of these expatriates that struck Elizabeth, but their commitment to assisting people they didn't know, something "which was not known to our people at that time". Elizabeth's excitement about the new life at The Grail was matched with a wider excitement that cut across this small central African country that was fizzing with optimism and hope.

Independence saw Uganda in charge of its own destiny, its politicians eager to harness the country's rich natural resources and create a bright future from their places in their new, modern state. On the eve of independence, colonial Uganda was in many ways well equipped to embark on successful independent statehood.

As a British Protectorate – a territory not formally annexed but where the British Crown has power and jurisdiction – Uganda had large deposits of cobalt and copper and a rich agricultural sector, where 75 per cent of cultivated land was devoted to subsistence agriculture and the remainder to cash crops. This had enabled financial self-sufficiency and a degree of independence from Britain. Such was the power of Ugandan agriculture that between 1945 and 1960 Uganda's peasants paid over £118 million to the administration for the development of their country. For these reasons, comparative to other colonies, the life expectancy of Ugandans was high, literacy rates were good, medical services reasonable, and the country had a functioning road and communications system. Social issues around race, too, were not as deeply entrenched in Uganda as they were in former settler colonies – for instance, Africa's first native Catholic bishop, Joseph Kiwanuka, who was ordained in 1939, was the Archbishop of Rubaga.

Yet it was in the high offices of Ugandan politics, where the first cracks of political conflict would emerge that would see the country plunged into over 30 years of civil conflict and political persecution. Political strife would take the lives of over 1.5 million Ugandans, with the war tearing up much of the country's infrastructure as well as the social bonds that bound Ugandans to one another. Although Patricia did not know it at the time, she would go on to dedicate her life and all of her considerable personal wealth to supporting Ugandans to overcome the horrors that they were to face and the legacy that the country's conflicts bequeathed them.

Yet in 1964 in this new country, there was much to be done. High levels of maternal mortality and infection meant that for the vast majority of Ugandan women giving birth and caring for newborn babies were fraught with danger. While in Britain Patricia was able to secure a job as a social worker at Uganda's Child Welfare and Adoption Society (CWAS). This organisation had been founded by Father Rawlinson in 1958 at the urging of the Catholic bishops of Uganda during the increase in missionary activity in the 1950s. Rawlinson was at the time the secretary-general of the Uganda Episcopal Conference, and in charge of the Catholic Secretariat's health and social services department. The society began life in the archdiocese of Kampala with the aim of providing a better future for the city's vulnerable, orphaned children by providing them with good care and protection, yet, in part due to the lack of government services, it was soon realised that children throughout the country needed care, and so the society expanded nationwide.

It did not take Patricia long to discover a fundamental lesson about the particular challenges facing the vast majority of parents in Uganda:

> Babies were often abandoned in hospitals when their mothers died in child birth, but I soon discovered that most of the "orphans", in fact, had families who, once the babies had got past the breast feeding

stage, were perfectly capable of looking after the children themselves. ...

In later years, Patricia gave a short presentation to younger members of her extended family, describing her work with the society:

> I had the most fascinating job imaginable –
> if you like that sort of thing. Lots of Catholic
> missions all over Uganda had a few
> orphans in their care. There still is a high
> maternity death rate in Uganda. Most
> mothers have their babies in the villages or
> come to hospitals far too late when the old
> women's native medicine hasn't done the
> trick in a complicated delivery. If the baby
> survives, the poor father has a problem
> since there may be no one to breast feed the
> baby. He may get a relative to take the child
> and feed it with a bottle, but then the baby
> usually dies within a few weeks of
> gastro-enteritis because the bottles are not
> kept clear of infection. More often the father
> disappears and leaves the baby in the
> hospital, where he knows it will be cared
> for by the sisters. The father may well stay
> lost until the child is about 14 or 16, when a
> boy is old enough to work or a girl is old
> enough to marry and produce a bride-price.
> Then he may come to claim the child.
> Meanwhile, he is convinced that he has
> made the best possible arrangement for his
> child's upbringing, ensuring that he gets

European care and schooling at no cost to himself – provided he keeps out of the way.

Unfortunately, these children grow up in a very unreal world with little contact with the village and relatives. They don't learn how to bring up a family through growing up in a family themselves. They tend to grow up as misfits in society and many, in desperation because they have known no other life, become priests and nuns when they grow up.

When Patricia arrived, CWAS had a small, shabby babies' home situated at Nsambya, on a hill towards the south side of Kampala, and provided services to missions and hospitals up and down the country. Patricia's role was to co-ordinate CWAS's child welfare and adoption operations. At the centre of her work for CWAS was the dilemma: how do I best care for this child? Her response was nearly always that children should be with their families. As she wrote ten years later, in a letter home: "My job was to trace the relatives of these children and to persuade them to have their children home."

In providing care to young babies and children, Patricia had to have a close working relationship with the law, and as a matter of course was often in the magistrates' court. A formidable woman, Matilda Ssengooba, was a magistrate at Kampala Juvenile court, later renamed the Family and Children's Court. To enter officially into the care of the society, every child that was abandoned had to be brought before the court to 'know the circumstances', at which point Ssengooba or another magistrate would make the necessary court order placing the children in the care of the society.

"That lady has surprised me. She would know each and every child," Ssengooba recounted of Patricia. These legal proceedings were no mere formality, as the social worker needed to demonstrate that he or she had thoroughly investigated the child's circumstance. This meant finding the origins of the child's family: a real challenge as in many cases children were simply abandoned by the dusty roadsides outside mission stations. Patricia went about this task with her usual gusto, placing advertisements and announcements in national newspapers such as the Catholic daily the *Munno*. Advertisements, which she paid for herself, were published both in English and local languages and would be distributed around the country. In her own words:

> Finding the relatives of the children was often quite exciting and took me to every corner of the country, into towns, plantations, remote villages; it sometimes even involved following a nomadic family group to wherever they were currently grazing their cattle.

This meant travelling up and down the country – to the green fertile plains of Gulu and regions north of the Nile, to the areas around the town of Tororo near the Kenyan border, and as far as the terraced mountains of the South where Uganda met with the Congo and Rwanda.

Initially, Patricia travelled by any means necessary – usually large *matatu* buses – but after a few years she bought a small Volkswagen Beetle to zip around in. This was an immense responsibility for a young woman in a country that was not her own. Indeed, Elizabeth Namaganda's admiration for Patricia was because of her humanity and determination to help people from a completely foreign culture, who spoke a different language, and lived in impoverished circumstances. Elizabeth reflected:

> At that time, many of our people didn't even read or write... She had to learn the language at work... That kind of humility, that kind of commitment to come to work with our people, to give a service where you don't relate much, and perhaps where you won't be much understood, is not a simple task.

The young Patricia was acutely aware of this difficulty, and the importance of the need to absorb culture and background. In a talk she gave 20 years later, she reflected:

> It's amazing to think that people from a totally different part of the world should presume to be able to sort out the lives of people who live so very differently from themselves. So many things are different:

the countryside, the climate, the people, the family structure, the traditions, the expectations people have of their lives. There was so much to learn and I was very fortunate that I was working in an all-African set-up. I was the only European working directly for the Child Welfare and Adoption Society although there were one or two European committee members and so I always had Ugandan colleagues who could interpret, not only the language, but also the real meaning of things, the customs and background to the problems we dealt with...

While exciting, once relatives were found, they were often in a particularly difficult situation. Loss of family, dysfunctional relationships, illegitimate children, and poverty – there were many reasons why babies and children were abandoned. "It could be very difficult", admitted Patricia in her talk to younger family members in 1974, "to understand Ugandans' cultures and advise parents on some of their most personal issues and encourage them to take their children back. I had to persuade people that children would be better off brought up in the poor homes of their relatives than in the comparative luxury but isolation of the mission compound."

Although Patricia was adamant that a child's best chances were with their own family, if a child's family could not be found or they were really unable to look after the child, then she would find African foster parents for them, which wasn't easy. Foster care involved the foster parents receiving a financial stipend from the government for the care of the child. This brought with it the obvious problem of people thinking more about money for themselves than looking after a child. It was Patricia's remit to ensure that every child was suitably placed with foster parents who looked after them, and then to report back to the family court after a three-month trial period. Patricia provided not only reports on the child, but also tried to support the foster parents. She would often teach foster parents, who were typically from poorer backgrounds, how they could work – either through sewing or simple jobs – and earn money to provide for their family.

"She was a very compassionate woman", remembers Ssengooba. "She ensured every child was happy in their location... She was determined to see that everything was working out, and would follow each detail meticulously. She'd ask, 'How is Monica doing?' etc. Her memory for names was excellent."

* * *

Back at 'Holmwood', Patricia's letters arrived with reasonable frequency, telling stories of child welfare and adoption and her adventures in Africa. To her parents, they seemed a world away from their heartfelt plans of her settling down into a life of marriage and motherhood. Rather, in one correspondence with her family and another with her long-time friend, Rosie Talbot, not long after she had arrived, she recounted what began as a beautiful recent hiking holiday, reminiscent of her younger holidays in Bavaria. She and a few friends, including a priest, had taken some days off to travel to the east of the country, to the green hilly outcrops which lie to the south of the vast Karamoja plains, to climb to the summit of Mount Elgon, an isolated and extinct volcano and Africa's eighth highest mountain. The landscape was stunning. Verdant green slopes were criss-crossed with waterfalls that cut through high red volcanic rocks, the most dramatic of which being the majestic Sipi Falls which plunge to the lower slopes of the mountain's foothills. The climb, steep though not too strenuous, was long and it took two days to reach the summit. Unlike in Bavaria, however, the priest with whom she was travelling came down with a malarial fever half way through the walk. He failed to make the final ascent, and when the group came back to the camp, they found that he had succumbed to the virus and died. Panic set among the camp, and the porters fled, leaving Patricia and her friend alone. With no other options available, they had to carry the corpse for two days as they made their way back down the mountain. "Never a dull day in Africa", Father De Reeper once wrote in a letter to Patricia. It certainly felt like that to Patricia's family and friends back home in Europe.

Despite her humble and frugal life in Uganda, Patricia began to realise that her family's financial resources could be a powerful tool. Taught never to boast, she was almost embarrassed by her family's wealth, and yet here in Uganda, away from the comforts that she had experienced when growing up, she realised that not only her labour but her money was needed to overcome some of the challenges that Ugandans around her faced. One of the most important of these, and one of her most long-lasting achievements with CWAS, was the professionalisation of their service. This began, as Patricia described during her family presentation in 1974, when "I had to set up more professional baby homes for orphans where they would be cared for by trained staff and where we could prepare the relatives from the start for the return of their babies when they were toddling and able to eat solid food." In doing this she spent months persuading her father to invest in a new purpose-built babies' home. He eventually agreed, and the Nsambya Babies Home, which had been founded in 1958, was redesigned as a functional, solid building built for the specific intention of housing these babies. It continues today.

Another difficulty that Patricia found was that "the other African social workers and sisters would often become attached to these children. They would want to mother them". Patricia's answer was to instil a deep culture of professionalism within the baby homes and CWAS, ensuring sisters and nurses offered care within limits and without getting too attached. These homes were to be, as she describes in a letter she wrote to her parents:

> ...run by sisters and nursery nurses to care
> for the very young babies while we were

contacting the relatives, building up their
confidence in their ability to care for the
child and then helping them when the baby
was first returned to their care.

The changes that Patricia made to CWAS, and her
continuing support after 1980, ensured that the society
flourished. Marking its 50th anniversary in 2008, the
society celebrated the support it had offered to
thousands of children in the years from 1958 to 2008
and Patricia was personally thanked by the society's
chairman, J.C. Ssempebwa, for her "continued
motherly assistance towards the needy children in our
hands".

Yet, despite her strict professionalism, Patricia herself
had an emotional impulse to care for the children she
worked with. John Kasule, a social worker at CWAS
as well as a friend, reflected: "Patricia took a very
strong stance not to be bonded [to children in her care],
but found it very difficult to break that bond." She
would often personally provide school fees or
financial support to orphans who did not have the
means. One such relationship was with a smart, yet
poor boy called Byekwaso Aloysius, who after
receiving care from Patricia at CWAS was hoping to
attend secondary school.

In a letter to Patricia in 1968, Byekwaso tells how he
had just been offered a place in one of Uganda's
premier schools, St. Mary's, Kisubi. Many of the

children at this school had families to support them, yet the teenage Byekwaso recounted:

> I have used the 10p out of my 20p for pocket money to buy some books but what I have bought is nothing because the books add up to almost 56p so now I am completely stuck because without books I can do nothing... And for clothing I use those clothes which the society gives me at the end of every year as a Christmas gift. Since you went not even a single relative of mine never visits me, simply because they doubt that their brother (my father) is my father.

Patricia intervened, although she impressed on the young Byekwaso that he must study hard. In a subsequent letter, Byekwaso proudly recounted his school marks – 550 marks out of 800 and a class ranking of 15th out of 32. He was achieving but made a promise to work harder. In a painfully neat, hand-written letter, he began:

> Dear Benefactress

> I am rather happy to write you this letter which I am going to tell you my marks for the first term and the second too. I think you will excuse me to use this word 'benefactress' as you told me not to use it, but I am right to use it because if it were not you I would not get any benefactor to give me money so in this way it is really you

who gives me money. I am told that my fees for next year have already arrived, so I thank you very much indeed, this means that I am very much thought of.

Patricia's close bonds with many of the children that she cared for brought pain as well as joy into her life. For personal successes such as Byekwaso getting to school, there were also tragedies. A particularly painful case was the story of Lillie Millie.

On the 13 April 1967, the bodies of two young girls were found stuffed into a sack floating in the Athi River near Nairobi, Kenya. While Patricia was back in England having a break at 'Holmwood', one of the girls she had cared for at CWAS and for whom she was providing school fees, had gone missing. Lillie Millie was a very pretty, mixed race young woman of 17, who wore her hair in a short afro. She had skipped school two weeks earlier and left with her 21 year-old friend, Sarah Massa, to go to Nairobi, ostensibly to get a job with East African Airlines. The girls had secretly left Kampala and taken a bus to Kenya where they stayed at a cheap hotel on one of Nairobi's main roads. A few days later they were seen in the morning coming out of the Kenyan Cinema building. This was the last time anyone saw them alive.

A friend of Patricia, who was keeping an eye on Lillie, wrote to her a week later to inform her of the news: "I was at the school and did not know of her going to Nairobi. I did not even know she was missing. I was only told by a student who read the newspaper." The devastating story was widely publicised in both the Ugandan and the Kenyan press. The bodies of Lillie and Sarah were flown back to Kampala by the Ugandan police, and from there the police took Lillie's body back to Nsambya, where, according to Patricia's friend, "the police also helped us dig the grave". Then, he continued:

> The coffin was opened when it reached home. Her body was white and black in some parts. It was swollen and her face was swollen, too. The hair on her head had gone off because of the long stay in the water and one could hardly recognise her. She was buried late that day in Nsambya grave yard.

Sniffer dogs were brought in as part of a joint Kenyan and Ugandan police manhunt up the riverside, which eventually resulted in finding and charging four men with the murders.

* * *

While Patricia was working with CWAS, dangerous political developments had begun to take hold of the country. Tensions had been growing between the prime minister, Milton Obote, and the president, Kabaka Muteesa II, as the challenges of running the multi-ethnic country began to give way to a hardening of political positions by the two leaders. In 1966, Father Kiggundu's *Munno* and other newspapers began publishing stories about the prime minister and a colonel of the Uganda Rifles regiment illegally smuggling gold out of neighbouring Zaire. Pressure increased against Obote and a parliamentary investigation was launched. Obote's response was swift. With the support of senior members of the armed forces, on 22 February Obote arrested five of his cabinet ministers, suspended the constitution, assumed all executive powers and removed Muteesa II from office.

Four years after independence the promise of Uganda was shaken. Over the next two months, the military and state security services increased their pressure against the Kabaka, who eventually fled the country in late May. In the face of escalating violence and uncertainty, the now 27 year-old Patricia came under pressure from her family to leave Uganda, which she did in late April. She wrote a hurried letter to Father De Reeper, her East African mentor, to inform him of her departure. In his response, he thanked her for the letter "which I received on the same day as alarming rumours concerning happenings in Kampala". He continued:

> I am worried and anxious to know whether you managed to get away in time before a clampdown was imposed on all traffic in and out of Kampala. I have tried to get telephonic contact with The Grail at Rubaga, but we cannot get through yet. I do hope sincerely that you have arrived safely and that you found everybody well at home.

Patricia did arrive safely back at 'Holmwood', but once the intensity of the political crisis had died down she returned to Uganda and to her role at CWAS, though Uganda had changed dangerously. The rule of law had begun to ebb away under Obote's increasingly authoritarian rule, political opponents were being tortured, there were food shortages, and corruption at all levels of government was increasing.

In a hint of prophetic irony, Father De Reeper had finished his 1966 letter: "I wonder what the next surprise will be!" In truth, it came just over two years later, at the end of January 1971. Milton Obote was in Singapore at a Commonwealth Heads of Government Meeting, when the head of the army, Idi Amin, ordered mechanised army units into strategic locations in Kampala and Entebbe, ending Obote's rule and installing himself as president. Amin's triumph was initially welcomed by many across the country. Yet it would turn out be one of the most bloody in the country's history, and would change the face of Uganda.

Patricia had again been forced to leave Uganda before Amin took power. At 32, she left the country she had come to love, and with it her work in Africa as a social worker. She would dedicate the rest of her life towards helping the people of Uganda and regularly visit, yet never again would she live so intimately and humbly with the people of the country. She reflected later in her presentation to younger family members:

That was probably the most happy and rewarding time of my life and I was in Uganda for nearly five years all told. In many ways it is a very unsettling experience, working in a developing country. One's values are turned upside down. You see so much real poverty, starving, sick children, lepers, and people with terrible disabilities, so many bright young people with no hope of ever getting decent work, and yet I have found nothing more peaceful than walking through a rural African village, seeing people who have no wealth working the land and making use of everything it can produce. The people seem contented. This is where modern Africans who go to the cities to work return to refuel their emotional and physical batteries in order to cope with the crazy way of life wealth imposes on us. It's rather idyllic... One's own wealth becomes quite unreal when viewed against the way people manage to live quite decent lives even though they have nothing.

Chapter IV

Return to England and new challenges

When Patricia returned to England from Uganda in late 1970, she yearned to keep up her contact with Africa. She "missed Uganda dreadfully for a long time" and her love for the country, and the wider continent, had a great influence on her hunt for a job. She found a job at the Commonwealth Students' Children Society (CSCS) which had been under the umbrella of the London Council of Social Service since 1968. The Council had begun to show concern over the issue of race relations in 1954 after an investigation into the facilities available to foreign students living within the district of Paddington in central London. The council aimed to confront the problems faced by immigrants living within indigenous British communities and to offer assistance to overcome these problems whenever this seemed possible. The CSCS played a pivotal role, dealing with students from Commonwealth countries who had come to Britain to further their education with their children in tow.

During her time with the CSCS – six years between 1971 and 1977, with two of them as head of the social work department – Patricia worked mostly with students from West and Southern Africa. These students faced extreme difficulties in securing adequate accommodation and child care for their families while they were studying. The West Africans came with deep-rooted aspirations, thrilled that they had gained entrance into a hallowed British university and excited to be abroad for their prestigious period of further study. Education is prized in West Africa; it is seen as the route to an improved life, accession to the status of one of the admired professionals working and helping provide for entire extended families.

Patricia herself says that she "learned a great deal about the needs and aspirations of these overseas families"; her time with them offered a valuable insight into their lives. The cultural gulf, between themselves and the British people and institutions that they came across, made itself known largely through the issue of fostering and adoption. Patricia's time at the CWAS in Uganda proved highly useful in discovering differing attitudes to adoption and she was able to help various West African families through their struggles with the British system of child care.

The far more communal society in West Africa differed greatly from that which the students found in Britain. The Kenyan theologian, John Mbiti, famously wrote that in East and West Africa familial and broader communal society revolves around the central axiom of "I am because we are and, since we are, therefore I am". The importance of the community over the individual offers a far more communally based view of the world, contrasting the European and American cult of the individual and the focus on the nuclear family. It is strong relationships with a variety of other people within a given community which offers meaning and significance in life.

This outlook also has a crucial consequence for child care in West Africa. June Ellis, an academic specialising in social work, discovered, when researching her edited volume *West African Families in Britain: A Meeting of Two Cultures*, a doctor from Ghana who said: "I have many mothers". The raising of a child is not restricted to that of the nuclear family and is far more of a collective effort. Ellis writes that the term 'brother' can be used not just for biological brothers but can also "include cousins and other distant connections of the same generation", and to add slight confusion it can also be "loosely used to refer to anyone of approximately the same age group". The term 'family' thus has connotations for a West African that strongly differ from those conjured up by a British usage of the term, which caused confusion for the West African students with whom Patricia worked.

The differences became most noticeable in the case of child care, stemming again from diverging meanings lurking behind the same word. Terms such as 'mother' would have varying meanings depending on whether they were uttered by either a West African or British person. Ellis found that a child might call their aunt or grandmother 'mother' because "she is the woman with whom the child has been most closely brought up": the "title can freely be given to a number of women without causing any confusion". Ellis even offers a word of caution to the social worker who might hear the phrase "you are my mother": this should be taken as a compliment and should not cause the social worker to descend into being concerned about dependency.

Most West African students with whom Patricia worked at the CSCS in the 1970s displayed a deep sense of respect and affection but she still encountered innumerable difficulties due to this cultural difference. Many Africans incorrectly saw in the private fosterers – people taking care of children as part of an unregulated and informal arrangement with the biological parents, with no involvement from the local authority – some intimation of their idea of the extended family fostering that they were used to back home.

In 2001 Terry Philpot, in *A Very Private Practice: An Investigation into Private Fostering*, could still write:

> It is also the case, as one study has shown, that many African parents had a mistaken view of white families with whom they placed their children. They believed that private fostering was like another version of their own culture of the extended family. But added to this they had a perception of white society that was, by definition,

educated and thus in these families the children could thrive educationally because of access to books and the like. The fact was that many of the receiving families were poor, motivated by wanting to make some pin money, would never have gained registration with a local authority, had a poor education themselves, and it was unlikely that there would be a book in the house. They were also very often completely ignorant of the child's home culture in even small but important matters like hair care and the child would often be living on out-of-town estates where there was not a black face to be seen.

Patricia saw negative aspects and potential dangers in many of these instances when recalling the situations that she tried to improve. She felt that many "resorted to fostering their children with English families, unaware of the different expectations of the foster family". This shows that fostering in Britain was fraught with problems – the families had to foster because child care was too expensive; or they resorted to fostering as a last-ditch effort to find affordable care for their child, or care that was convenient for them as they studied. A baby sitter or child minder would only offer expensive care for the working hours of the week, while a foster parent would offer prolonged care, allowing the students to study and also gain employment in the evening. This solution was not, however, ideal: the lack of cultural knowledge and the fact that they were unaware of what this kind of fostering truly meant in Britain, resulted in arguments and court cases where Patricia's department at the CSCS had to help the largely West African student parents.

Official fostering in Britain was (and is) carried out through local authorities and voluntary bodies but they were mostly unwilling to offer foster carers for children who still had parents able to care for them. The West African students longed for the extended family of home that could care for their children while they were studying. The public British system would not offer them anything remotely similar or workable and they were forced to turn to private foster homes with no regulation or safeguards.

By 1977, as many as 6,000 West African children were living in private foster homes in Britain. Without registration or regulation (as is still largely the case), private fostering leaves children open to those who have had no background checks and who have not proved that they are capable of providing adequate care for a child. There is always the risk of a potentially abusive private foster parent whose activities would go completely unchecked. It would not be too hard for such a foster carer to display an acceptable environment for the parent to observe when visiting only to descend into horrific treatment behind closed doors. In addition, often, visiting could not be frequent because the children would be placed at a considerable distance from where their parents were living.

There were other problems, too: a West African would never see the fostering of a child as something permanent but a British private foster carer might harbour the hope of keeping the child. Courtrooms were frequently the arenas where these problems were fought out and the judges more often ruled in favour of the British foster carers.

The ease with which private fostering could be carried out was also disturbing. In her chapter 'Private Fostering', in Ellis's *West African Families in Britain*, Vivien Biggs (who also worked at the CSCS in the 1970s), sums up this rapid process: "An advertisement is answered, the parents visit, she [the carer] lays down her terms, and (if they agree) the child soon arrives."

The calculating exchange – an advertisement bringing commodified child care with rapidity and ease – seems far removed from controlled, safe foster care processed through a local authority acting as the supportive third party. With official fostering, the local authority takes due time and consideration to handle the arrangement. A social worker makes many visits to the potential foster home, all the time evaluating both the home and the motives of the prospective foster parent. References are sought, the applicant's suitability for the role is meticulously considered so that foster carers can be approved and a good home found for children. An attempt is also made to match carer and child. The social worker must also frequently visit the foster home where the child lives to check whether the appropriate care is being offered and also to check that a workable arrangement exists between the foster family, the child's biological parents (where continued contact is appropriate), and the fostered child. None of this occurs in private fostering, which puts children in these foster homes in a potentially harmful environment.

For these reasons, Patricia campaigned against private fostering throughout her seven years at the CSCS. She and the Society urged the government to ban the practice of private fostering, arguing that inestimable problems emerged from the lack of regulation and registration.

While Patricia was working at the CSCS, the Society would answer advertisements placed by people seeking private foster homes in parenting magazines. This preventative measure involved offering counselling to these parents, advising them against potentially damaging private arrangements and also requesting that the parents forward the details of anyone who answered their advertisements. At the Society, Patricia aimed to support African families through many difficult situations offering advice in order to help African parents and British foster carers bridge the gap between their misunderstandings.

Patricia deems this period of her working life as highly important in the development of her views and aspirations. She considers that her seven years with the CSCS broadened her horizons as she was able more deeply to understand the issues facing West African students with children in Britain. The most common dilemma sprang from being used to a culture in which various people would play a role in raising a child. This became particularly apparent when the West African parents would decide to take back the child. They often could not understand the possessive, tight bond that many foster carers made with their child. While the care of a child might be shared at home in West Africa, the importance of the biological parents would never be forgotten. With legal adoption very much part of society in Britain, the British foster carers would see it as perfectly possible for a fostered child eventually to end up as their adopted child. Thus the two sets of parents approached the matter from completely differing standpoints stemming from the perspectives of their respective societies.

Patricia encountered these intensely personal and emotionally fraught issues while working for the CSCS. When the matter of the return of a foster child to their biological parents arose some cases ended in tragedy for the latter. With close bonds created within the British foster family, and the child used to their care during formative years, many children did not wish to return to their biological parents. A familiar home would always seem preferable to one that is unknown. The very fact of their placement in the former might even lead them to question the adequacy of the latter. At the time, one judge presiding over a case brought against a British foster family by Ghanaian parents accepted as evidence the nine year-old girl's letter pleading for her stay in Britain. This case, with the girl referred to in the press at the time as simply "Ann from Ghana", ended with the child being kept in Britain by her British foster carers. She had been raised as a British child with no link to her cultural heritage and making a trip to Ghana, to live with parents who were effectively strangers to her, seemed unpalatable. Once the judge gave the verdict that the child should stay with her foster carers in Britain, her biological mother stormed across the court room and hit the foster mother in her face screaming: "You will die; you have broken up my home". Such strong emotion and keenly felt anguish was only to be expected in such an intimate struggle.

Those working at the CSCS encountered numerous cases such as this. There were many horror stories of possessive British parents who raised their fostered West African children without ever enlightening them about their heritage. They were encouraged to think of themselves as fully British children and were often taught to fear the black identity of their parents and overlook and erase their own identity. In Britain, the breath of fascists and racists lingered long in the air, and the issue of being a black child in a society where racism was sometimes not far from the surface cannot be overlooked. Unflattering depictions in the right wing media fuelled by racist rhetoric all combined to make Britain a prejudiced place in which to grow up. The white foster carers could demonise the black parents, conjuring awful images and planting deep-rooted fears. These West African children would also be more used to the parenting style of their British foster carers and were often taught to fear that of their biological parents.

Unregulated private fostering was fraught with problems and Patricia and the CSCS thought that at least ensuring some registration and regulation of private fostering would help to alleviate some of the issues that arose. She also held the deep-seated belief that a firm line of contact had to be established and maintained with the biological parents. She learnt this early at the CWAS in Uganda, which placed a focus upon the need to locate a child's natural parents. If this approach was maintained, then some of the cultural clashes occurring between West Africans and British foster carers could be avoided, or at least some of the destructive impact might be sanded down. A child knowing that its biological parents were black West Africans who aimed to take him or her back to West Africa in the future would feel less shocked by this eventual situation. Moreover, this knowledge would help the child to understand fully his or her identity – feelings of displacement might be inevitable, but feelings of alienation might be avoided. A child who grew up in a white British foster home in which his biological parents' culture was explained, maintained and celebrated would be far more likely to be able to move smoothly back to West Africa with his or her biological parents. Yet whatever the efforts of Patricia and the CSCS to alleviate the situation, the fact remains that 40 years later many of these problems remain and private fostering still remains largely unregulated.

Patricia's time at the CSCS proved formative and helped her to decide the direction of her future work.

Through working with African students newly arrived in Britain, she was able to discuss exactly what their needs and aspirations might involve. She discovered, after these prolonged conversations, that a professional service would be of prime importance in all the developing countries. She recognised, too, that her beloved but war-torn Uganda would be especially needy after losing so many of their intelligentsia to the war. This all stemmed from her close conversations with African students at the society. These provided the seeds for her eventual foundation of the Kulika Trust to offer student scholarships to study at British universities, initially for students from Commonwealth countries.

So many matters had come to Patricia's attention in the seven years she had spent at the CSCS, many of which had an impact on the happiness of children, their education and their relationship with their biological parents. She now saw that if she was to have a more lasting effect and one that was to be actually directed by her, then she had to strike out in a new direction. Education struck her as crucial and she was keen to find ways of making the experience of studying while having children more pleasant and workable. And so it was that she left the society. The thoughts and experiences that she had gathered in those years were working within her as she returned to Post Box Cottage, next door to Warren Farm in Berkshire, and it was here, in 1978, that a new chapter of her life would unfold.

* * *

Patricia aged 3
in the nursery
at her home in
Mettingen

Patricia on her way to Perugia

Patricia's graduation from
St Andrews University

Patricia as a young social worker in Uganda

Patricia with life-long friend Gerda Roumen and a priest friend of the Grail

Beatrice and her family with Patricia

Patricia and Andrew Jones with members of the Child Welfare and Adoption Society and Nsambya Babies Home

A group of children residing at Nsambya Babies Home

Patricia outside
Post Box Cottage
with her dog
Scampi and
children from
Warren Farm

Patricia and her good friend Sally with children from Warren Farm

Games in the garden at Warren Farm

Birthday celebrations at Warren Farm

The Grail sisters in Kampala in the 1980s

The famous Beetle that Patricia drove around Uganda, parked at the Grail

Elizabeth Namaganda and Adrian Sibo, Kulika's first Board members

Basil Kiwanuka and Rev Canon David Sentongo, Kulika's first Board members

Rev Canon David Sentongo's daughter with Nightingale Kalinda,
friend to Patricia and Kulika

Sym Kiwanuka (First CEO of Kulika), Basil Kiwanuka, Brian Evans (Kulika UK)
and Dr WR Makuza (Kulika beneficiary, Head of the Civil Aviation Authority
and Trustee of Kulika Uganda)

Patricia with Basil Kiwanuka and Berna Kiwanuka

Warren Farm as a training centre for Sustainable and Organic Farming

Elijah Kyamuwendo, one of the first two farmers who came to Warren Farm in 1991 to train in Organic and Sustainable Agriculture. Elijah became the second CEO of Kulika Uganda

Josephine Kizza, one of the first two farmers who came to Warren Farm in 1991 to train in Organic and Sustainable Agriculture

Rev Canon David Sentongo, Elijah Kyamuwendo and Sym Kiwanuka

Members of Kulika Uganda

David and Annette Barker, Andrew Jones, Patricia, Sue Errington and
Alastair Taylor with Kulika trained farmers, and Kulika tutors

Patricia accepting a thank you gift from a group of Kulika beneficiaries

Professors from the Open University together with graduates of the MA in development management, and a member of the Kulika Board

Andrew Jones and Patricia giving a speech at the party to celebrate the handover of the farmer training programme from the UK to Uganda

A Kulika farmer and her family preparing an evening meal

Kulika farmers preparing a meal on their fuel-saving stove,
built as a result of Kulika's training

Edith Nakatudde, beneficiary of the food security project in Nakasongola,
weeding cabbage with her grandchildren during school holidays

Children weeding a potato garden at Kanyogoga Primary School, Mubende
under the Food For Thought Project

Martin Sematimba and Florence Namulindwa on a support visit to
CADeP farms in Western Uganda

Kulika Uganda Team 2007

Patricia with the Hon James Baba (left), Minister of State in the Office of the
Vice President at Kulika's 25th Anniversary celebrations held at Lutisi

Patricia planting a tree at the Kulika Training Centre
in commemoration of 25 years of Kulika

The Patricia wing at the Kulika Training Centre at Lutisi.
This is the building for female accommodation

Patricia, Elijah Kyamuwendo and Professor Senteza Kajubi,
giving a lecture at Makerere University to celebrate 25 years of Kulika

Credit: Madeleine Lustigman

Patrica tasting wine made by Kulika beneficiary and Grail Sister also called Patricia

Credit: Kulika Uganda

Francis Magara, Kulika Key Farmer Trainer taking Patricia around a Kulika farm

Patricia and Madeleine Lustigman together with Norah Bwaya (First Chairperson) and John Kayondo (First Treasurer) of Ka Tutandike Uganda

A mother and market vendor at Kalerwe Market,who took part in Ka Tutandike's first early years programme based at Miles2Smiles Day Care Centre

Christine Semambo Sempebwa, Ka Tutandike's first CEO in Uganda, together with Catherine Kitongo, founder of Miles2Smiles Day Care Centre visiting a parent who worked in the nearby market

Heidi Kruitwagen and Anisha Rajapakse with Susan Kisitu, CEO of Ka Tutandike Uganda and staff members, Shamila and Jennifer

Heidi Kruitwagen with children from St Jude nursery school

Patricia with Hon Suleiman Madada, Minister of State for Disability and the Elderly Affairs in the Ministry of Gender Labour and Social Development, Hon Alex Ndeezi, Member of Parliament (representing PWDs in the Central region), Uganda's first deaf Member of Parliament and Executive Director, Uganda National Association of the Deaf, MP Nokrach William (representing PWDs in the Northern region), Prof Okoth Okombo, Professor of linguistics at Nairobi University, Richard Dowden (KTTUK Trustee) and Heidi Kruitwagen and Anisha Rajapakse

Women vendors from the Nakawa market with their children at the
Nobles Day Care Centre

Patrica with her friend Carol O'Donnell and Jane Leek when they visited Uganda
in August 2012 to pay their respects on the death of Elizabeth Namaganda and
Elijah Kyamuwendo

Elizabeth Namaganda was a social worker and a member of the Uganda branch of the international lay organisation, The Grail, where she met Patricia in 1970s. She travelled to Holland and the USA for further studies in social work, before returning to Uganda and becoming the head of the order of the sisters in Uganda. Patricia asked Elizabeth to be a board member of Kulika Uganda when the new organisation was established. She died in 2011.

I was a student and we saw each other from time to time because we were working in the same group. Patricia was a social worker, and I was also studying social work, and that brought me from time to time together with her. Patricia came as a volunteer to work with homeless, rejected children that were often left on the street. That kind of service among those sorts of people was not normal at that time. What I admired about Patricia as a young woman, was to see these women and the doctors and nurses, people of status and particularly Patricia, who I came to know later was from a well-to-do family, come to do social work here with people whose culture or language you don't share. That was really something. You have to really come down to give services that you want to give to the people. I am grateful to Patricia for what she did, and also for the family who upheld her support and her mission here. I wish this example to be taken on by many people, and also to be her legacy, and that it can be a future way of leading people to do something good for others. She deserves to be remembered.

* * *

John Harton Kasule is a social worker in Uganda and worked in the role Patricia occupied during her initial time in Uganda. He was responsible for much of the administration of the private financial support that Patricia continued to give several children and orphans, in addition to carrying out his professional social care commitments.

It was a blessing to work with Patricia Brenninkmeyer. I was recruited in 1989 by the Archdiocese of Kampala to work as a social worker for the Child Welfare and Adoption Society; a charity of the Catholic Church founded in 1958. Patricia had worked as a volunteer social worker for the NGO for several years before I joined. When Patricia visited the NGO in 1989 she found that I did the job well and as she used to do it, tracing relatives of abandoned, orphaned and displaced children for their reunion or for fostering them within Uganda. She got a good impression of my work and my love for needy children.

Patricia's great love for needy people drove her to share her financial and material resources and to give psychological support to people. She identified me to be her contact person in these areas. I monitored the persons she supported. She was another Mother Teresa of Calcutta of India.

I shall live to always remember that it was a great blessing to work with Patricia Brenninkmeyer and I thank God for that chance.

Chapter V

Life at Post Box Cottage: The creation of Warren Farm

In the way that she had chosen to live her life, Patricia had laid her own foundation stones – from developing her interest in Africa to gaining experience in children's homes; from working for the Child Welfare and Adoption Society in Uganda, to working for the Commonwealth Students' Children Society in England. Each one of her experiences fortified her and built up to the most natural subsequent step – to open a residential group home to meet the needs of the student parents and their children and avoid the dangers of the children's potential alienation from both their parents' and their heritage. Once she decided to leave the Commonwealth Students' Children Society in 1978, Patricia decided to open that home. Her "little cottage in Streatley" in Berkshire, as she described it, could hardly offer the space needed for such a venture but she jokes that "ample evidence of the existence of God" arrived in the form of a 'For Sale' sign being hammered into the front garden next door. This property was quite different from Patricia's own – it was a large farm house with attached stables and a barn set amid seven acres of land. Patricia's views on the property are still quite clear when she remarks that "it was absolutely perfect for my purpose". Opening the home brought with it its own challenges and the size of the undertaking quickly expanded: "I started off mostly with babies but then they grew – it all grew!" However, Patricia's over-riding feelings are clear to behold; her description of life at Warren Farm is simple – "it was lovely".

When her father died in 1976, Patricia received part of her inheritance. She was able to purchase the large property next door while she also kept her cottage. Charity was always a major focus for the family and Arnold Brenninkmeyer had always admired Patricia's dedication to her cause. She had the family's advisers at her disposal and could seek advice whenever it was required. However, colleagues have mentioned Patricia's lack of patience with bankers and accountants, combined with her determination not to be controlled. With the arrival of her inheritance, she could decide what to do with her funds and she acted with a characteristic independence of spirit. With her inherited money, she was granted far more freedom and her general response was informed, according to her brothers, by her view of life being a vocation by which "you don't win anything – the rewards come on the other side".

Patricia was adamant that she would spend her money, nurturing absolutely no desire to make her wealth grow. She conveyed her feelings about money to her brothers when she said: "At the end of my life I want it to be finished." She spent much of it on Warren Farm.

After buying Warren Farm Patricia had various alterations made. She intended to provide care for the children of Commonwealth students, while their parents studied. Patricia's seven years at the Commonwealth Student's Children Society had shown her the gaping hole in provision of this sort. It was sorely needed to avoid any of the painful fostering tangles that separated unwitting parents and their children. Central to Patricia's philosophy was the notion that the parental link must be kept strong with the child and this influenced her alteration plans for the newly acquired property.

The stables were (according to the farm's brochure issued to parents) converted into four bed-sitting rooms where families whose children were being cared for would be able to come and stay. There was also a cottage in the garden, with self-catering facilities. This ensured that parents leaving their children to be looked after during their period of study in Britain could visit whenever they wished – the crucial link between parent and child was thus retained and strengthened. Home comforts were provided – a communal kitchen with four separate cooking tops and ovens, and sitting room made this less of a hotel and more of a temporary home to be used during the university holidays. Moreover, the attractive environs of the local area, the rolling hills of the Berkshire countryside, meant that it proved an ideal holiday location for Commonwealth students to take time away from study and to reconnect with their children.

During these all-important visits, Patricia and her small group of staff still offered care and help to the parents of the children. They were free to explore the local area without their children if they so wished, leaving them with the staff at the home. Visiting parents would eventually return to their British universities, safe in the knowledge that their children were being carefully looked after. Thus, full care was given to the students' children, and Patricia was able to address a certain number of the wrongs she had witnessed at the CSCS. The children were only to be looked after for a period no longer than three years – corresponding with the length of a British degree course. They were then returned to their parents who would take them back to their home country. The ease of this handing back stood in stark contrast to some of the complicated and muddled private fostering arrangements which Patricia had previously fought against. It was her expertise and experience as a social worker and as the head of the social work department at the CSCS that enabled her to recognise that offering the parents accommodation and regular visits must be a key feature of her idiosyncratic and successful home.

The barn attached to the farmyard was also turned into the Streatley Nursery, which was a playgroup run for the local three to five year-olds. A small toddler group was also run in the main Warren Farm house on five mornings a week for children from the local area. The children of Streatley were thus able to use Patricia's excellent facilities. Her aim at the time was to not only offer a safe and caring environment but, in her own words, to "provide a lot of fun to a lot of people". Patricia clearly derived great enjoyment from her work and her response was marked by this strong desire to spread this joy throughout the local community. She wanted to share the facilities that she set up with various youth groups instead of focussing on just the children at Warren Farm. She also started a small farm with animals, partly for the sake of the children, but which would also provide eggs, milk, and meat for the kitchen and manure for the large vegetable garden. Her later focus on sustainable organic agriculture in Uganda was to have its seeds in this early feature of Warren Farm.

Warren Farm was described by the brochure as a "four-bedroomed thatched farm house", boasting "large well-furnished living rooms, and a very spacious playroom with French windows leading to a safe play area in the garden". The brochure highlights that Warren Farm provided a caring community of people skilled in child care with an emphasis on good understanding of child development. Warren Farm, importantly, offered help for families involved with foster care through support from local authority social workers who would construct, and help families to follow, a graduated programme for return home. This employment of others was essential to Patricia's work – she emerged as very much the manager not just the social worker. She became the chairman of the council of management and drew on her substantial skills as an experienced social worker. She employed a qualified nursery nurse and a housekeeper. She also gave a home to a retired gamekeeper named Frank who took care of the gardening. Here she showed support to someone struggling to find his way after a previous criminal conviction. She looked beyond his past in a way that other people might not have done and she supported him until his death. Patricia's thoroughly professional team was further augmented by Community Service Volunteers and other helpers from both home and abroad, each with their own gifts and playing an invaluable part in ensuring that her dream for Warren Farm was fulfilled.

Patricia's exploits made for an enlightening article in a local newspaper at the time that described the eventual Warren Farm annual summer play scheme as a source of "non-stop fun, games and laughter for the children". The positioning of Warren Farm made it the ideal setting for inquisitive children to go for long walks, picnics and for endless bike rides. Patricia and her staff certainly had their hands full with 25 children in the residential play scheme, with children who slept in the barn staying at Warren Farm for weeks during the summer holidays. Ten of these children came from local authority children's homes while the rest came from families whose parents were unable to cope with their children for the entirety of the lengthy summer holiday. Patricia kept this summer play scheme as a strictly play-orientated experience, recognising that the children were after all on their summer holiday. They were able to spend "all day, every day playing to their hearts' content".

In addition, a special weekly outing was arranged for the children with one of the favoured venues being Windsor Safari Park with its (among others) lions, tigers, bears, cheetahs, giraffes and elephants – many of which the children had never seen before. Slightly closer to home, The Child-Beale Park in Reading, Berkshire, offered similarly exotic (if somewhat smaller) animals in combination with more English farm animals and birds, as well as landscaped gardens, woodlands and children's play areas. Patricia saw the benefit of such outings to children who might not have had the chance to explore widely and who needed the freedom to devote time to pure enjoyment. She was confident in her viewpoint, telling the local paper at the time that "the children love it". In addition to the organised entertainment, Patricia felt that the play scheme gave all of the children involved the chance to build new friendships with other children. The success of this notion, and of the Warren Farm play scheme in general, was shown with perhaps the greatest compliment paid – many children happily returned over the following summers.

Patricia's play scheme thrived. At the time, Patricia said "we seem to have been very lucky" as the volunteers poured in. Her advertisements for volunteers resulted in a good response. Numbers were further bolstered by trainee teachers from schools in London keen to provide help. Patricia was pleased that others believed in the play scheme at Warren Farm and never failed to see it as a wholly new and exciting venture.

The Warren Farm bedsits formed from the converted stable buildings also came into use in 1978. After the first few families had a residential session over the Easter period, Patricia observed that "they certainly enjoyed themselves and benefitted from the experience". This mixture of usefulness and benefit, but at the same time maintaining a focus upon delight and pleasure, could arguably be deemed one of the defining features of Patricia's response to the work and purpose of Warren Farm. Words like "fun" and "enjoyment" repeatedly crop up in any of her discussions and written thoughts about Warren Farm; she was clearly creating something offering pleasure and joy, as well as stability and care. For Patricia, the provision of joy remained firmly front and centre, making Warren Farm a remarkable haven for the children whom she was able to take on and provide care for.

Warren Farm was certainly a unique group home being, as it was, fully informed by the reasons which underlay its foundation – a place where Commonwealth students could leave their children in safe and resolutely temporary care. She saw it as very much a continuation of her work in Uganda and, according to Brian Evans, the chief secretary of Warren Farm, one could not "underestimate the amount of good that she did". It was not only inspiring but also exciting. Patricia showed "no interest in money unless it could be used for good" and Warren Farm proved an expensive project. Patricia often speaks and writes about leaving her "heart in Uganda" but the events of the time – from the upheaval by, and subsequent removal of, Idi Amin through to the Ugandan Bush War – prevented her from being able to work directly in that country. Instead, the children of Ugandans, and of those from other Commonwealth countries, could still be helped through the group home at Warren Farm.

Some of the London-based social workers to whom the authors spoke have deemed Patricia's work "trailblazing". She worked during a period of great change in the world of social work. The Seebohm Report of 1968 concluded that the division of three local authority welfare departments – children's, welfare and mental health – was proving ineffective. The proposals of the report were implemented in 1970 and the three departments were amalgamated under the umbrella social services department, giving, as the Seebohm report wanted, "one door on which to knock". While some local authorities interpreted "generic" departments to mean that their social workers could take on the cases of any and all client groups, Seebohm had intended – and some other authorities ensured that this was so – that it was departments, not the social workers' caseloads, that were generic.

Qualifications were less common at this time than they have since become – it is now mandatory to hold a social work qualification and be registered by the regulatory authority, the Health and Social Care Professions Council. Yet, at the time of the Seebohm reforms, there were still many social workers who had started work before the Second World War and had come from a variety of backgrounds, sometimes working themselves up from administrative jobs. But even for the younger members – those who had come in after the Second World War – while many were graduates, entry to social work did not depend on a university degree, as it does now. However, many of these social workers gained qualifications like the Home Office Certificate in Child Care or, like Patricia, held a degree in applied social studies, and their successor qualifications.

Patricia's training at the University of Liverpool would have set her slightly apart from other social workers who did not have the benefit of a university qualification – she could offer a wealth of expert knowledge and highly applicable skills. It gave her the opportunity to conduct work that was, as deemed by London social workers at the time, "so impressive and unique with a rare lack of focus on a Eurocentric approach". They see this latter view as having a "blinding effect that prevents one from seeing things from a different perspective". Patricia was regarded as "decidedly different, clued up" and, more importantly, "well ahead of her time to have such a deep respect for Ugandan values".

The period in which she was working gave her the freedom to achieve what she wanted within social work. She was free to help at least some of the problems that she discovered through her work at the CSCS. From the 1960s to early 1980s, large voluntary bodies like Barnardo's, the National Children's Home (later NCH and now Action for Children) and the Children's Society, and also small voluntary bodies like the Catholic children's societies, certainly had no specifically African focus, other than children of African descent who might come into their care. This was an issue that Patricia was keen to rectify when she set up Warren Farm as a group home for families in need.

The stories from children that stayed at Warren Farm are overwhelmingly positive. Patricia was in contact with Nightingale Kalinda, an influential female physiotherapist in Uganda. Nightingale passed recommendations from Uganda to Patricia about young Ugandans who were in particular need of assistance. One such child was three year-old Juliet Nakayiiwa, from the town of Mityana, 77 kilometres west of the capital, Kampala. Juliet was taken ill as a child with polio which affected the growth of her hips. Nightingale presented Juliet's case to Patricia who decided to help. She flew the pair to England in order for Juliet to stay at Warren Farm and to have an operation to improve her condition. When Juliet left Warren Farm, Patricia gave her a scrap book which begins with the tale of Juliet's arrival at Gatwick in 1988. Patricia wrote in it that Juliet was with

Nightingale in the immigration office "looking rather lonely and forgotten because the immigration officer wouldn't let them into the country until someone had come to claim them". Patricia arrived and took the pair to Warren Farm.

Patricia ensured that a potentially jarring trip to a new temporary home in England was made more comfortable. Prior to their departure, she had asked Nightingale to stay with Juliet for two weeks to help the child acclimatise to a different life. At Warren Farm it was, according to Patricia's scrap book, "comforting to have Nightingale sleeping in the same room" with Juliet. Patricia acknowledged that "it was a little scary" coming down to breakfast next morning and meeting all the people who lived at Warren Farm. After all, "there were so many of them and they were all interested in the little girl from Uganda who couldn't walk or speak English". Patricia ensured that no problems arose. Everyone already at Warren Farm was affected by its congenial atmosphere and was very kind, meaning that Juliet made a few friends and learned a few words of English. Keen for Juliet to hold onto her cultural heritage, because, after all, she would eventually be returning to Uganda, Patricia encouraged her to teach the boys at Warren Farm a few words of Luganda, one of the Ugandan languages.

When Nightingale had to return to Uganda, Juliet was understandably upset and cried a bit but Patricia's understanding approach helped alleviate the situation. She suggested that Juliet slept with her family's picture under her pillow and kept reminding her about the many distractions at Warren Farm, the new clothes and a whole playroom full of toys and lots of children to play with. Trips to the beach and to Scotland followed, as did a typical English Christmas. Soon Patricia was able to state that "Juliet is getting really independent".

Patricia stayed with Juliet while she had her operation at the Nuffield Orthopaedic Centre in Oxford, and after a period of rehabilitation Juliet was able to return home to Uganda with her meticulously created scrap book in her bag, courtesy of Patricia. Patricia continued to visit Juliet and ensured that her house in Uganda was fitted with rails. She donated money for the building of a new house and Juliet now says that "all my life has been moving with Patricia; she has helped me a lot". Juliet's care at Warren Farm was extremely personal, and Patricia completely changed the course of Juliet's life.

Patricia herself recounts receiving Juliet as a "complete baby, an utter baby... I looked after her from the start – it was lovely." She continues: "We are still very close, Juliet and I, but she is now *grown up*." Her tone emphasises those last two words showing pride that one of the children she helped is now successful and comfortable in Uganda, with her own shop and house. Implicit, too, whenever she talks about Juliet, is an immersion in a fond memory of a girl she cared for intimately, helping her sleep by placing photographs beneath her pillow.

Whenever Patricia speaks of the children of Warren Farm her tone is tinged with nostalgia, even when describing one boy, "a very difficult boy" who, on the first day at a local school picked a fight with somebody and threw a chair through a window. He was sent away from school and by lunchtime he had returned to Warren Farm and was never accepted back at school again. Here Patricia not only had a difficult boy, but one who could not be allowed at school, so he needed occupying throughout the day. This seemingly stressful situation is simply described by Patricia with a smile. "That was quite a handful", she says, and can only describe him in quite charming terms as "an absolute mischief".

At Warren Farm, Patricia was able to help African students and their children and she says that she was very lucky to be able to provide this care in such a beautiful setting. With characteristic humility, she repeatedly states that there are lots more things that could be done, which coheres with her brothers' view that Patricia sees life as a vocation. She acknowledged that "it's very rare for a social worker to be able to do something positive about a problem that he [or she] has seen". Patricia had the means to fix a problem that she had seen experienced by Africans and other individuals from elsewhere in the Commonwealth. However, as the years progressed, Patricia became increasingly aware of the difference in age between herself and the staff, and given the regular changes of the cook and the nanny, she was coming to be seen more as an authority and less as a colleague – a position with which she was never comfortable.

Patricia stated, during the time when Warren Farm was being run as a residential home: "Here I am, with the money available, able to help in a very small corner of a huge problem. That seems to me the best use I can make of my privileged position given my background and training."

* * *

During her time at Warren Farm, Patricia had kept in close contact with and visited her disabled brother John. In fact, Patricia's close relationship with John began in 1983 when she built an extension to Post Box Cottage, at the foot of the drive to Warren Farm, to make a home for him. In the event, it was decided by the Brenninkmeyer family, for the benefit of all concerned, that John should move to a bungalow on the High Street in Goring, just across the Thames from Streatley. He lived there very happily until 1994 with his nurse, a friend of Patricia's from her earliest days in Uganda. John was a real constant in her life. His bungalow was on the way to the station and to the shops that most of the staff and children at Warren Farm visited daily. Patricia would call in with anyone she happened to have in tow. He greatly enjoyed these visits, which were also important for the nurse as a diversion from the fixed routine of the daily life at the bungalow necessitated by John's multiple disabilities.

The situation only changed when it became clear that John was too much for one person to handle 24 hours a day, seven days a week, without expert medical assistance to fall back on. This, combined with the nurse's advancing years, precipitated the move from Goring to Holy Cross Hospital in Haslemere run by Daughters of the Cross who specialised in the care of people with long-term and severe disabilities.

Again, John had his own bungalow adjoining the hospital where he and the nurse were supported medically, socially and spiritually by the sisters with great loving care until he died peacefully 12 years later, in 2006. During all that time Patricia would make the one and a half hour trek from Berkshire to visit him faithfully every Sunday evening.

Patricia and John's brother, Michael, a Jesuit priest, said that John was an "icon" in the family, using the word in its proper sense – someone or something through which others see that something deeper lies beyond. John lacked power, money, the ability to shape his own life or even the means to look after himself, and yet he was content, without a worry in the world. It was the small things in life – winding up of the grandfather clock, receiving postcards, seeing aeroplanes, passing traffic on the High Street, a visit from Patricia and the children from Warren Farm, or any one of his family – that made his day. Although unable to speak, he had a great memory for the kind things that people did for him and would reward them with an enthusiastic smile as he fished out just the postcard from the pile that that person had sent him and tried to re-read it to them.

Thus, he was truly iconic in that all who met him could see how little is really necessary for a happy and fulfilled life. This was a constant and salutary lesson for Patricia and all his family and, indeed, all who met him.

* * *

Nightingale Kalinda is an important figure in Uganda having spent her life helping those with disabilities through community-based rehabilitation schemes. She had a spell working for Action Aid and also played a pivotal role in introducing physiotherapy to Uganda. Once she established a relationship with Patricia, she used to refer children with special needs to her in order that they might be helped financially with operations, education and housing.

I call Patricia my sister. She was different. She had been in Uganda for a long time. I was impressed that she had done so much for Ugandans. She was very interested in my work. I wrote to her thanking her for her interest. After this I showed Patricia some cases that needed particular help and Patricia helped many people.

She sponsored disabled people in need to get training. She sponsored people with paraplegia, orthopaedic workshops and polio victims. And after this, when she visited Uganda, she always wanted to see what they had achieved after being sponsored. She would say: "Make sure the child uses the money and that when I come there is something to see." So I took her to the field to see what these young people had done and to meet their parents. I overloaded her with cases and she sponsored many of them.

I was the one who took Patricia to see results and I always said: "I do not want to cheat you if you want to see how your money has helped." Patricia would be very happy after all of these visits, to see her work and she would say: "I am so impressed". When I say that she is my sister – that is a touching status in my own mind. She was everything to me. We thought in a similar way, I always say: "Today is mine, tomorrow is someone else's, so do what you can".

* * *

Juliet Nakayiiwa was recommended to Patricia by Nightingale Kalinda as a child in great need of an operation to help with some of her disabilities associated with an early bout of polio. She lived with Patricia in England from the age of three to five. She currently owns a small shop in Masaka from which she sells stationery.

I made international friends through Patricia. I stayed with her at Warren Farm and travelled with her to Scotland and to see members of her family. She had seen a video of me taken by Nightingale Kalinda who was doing community-based rehabilitation and working with Action Aid. Nightingale looked after disabled people or those who had been affected by accidents. I am thankful for that day – it was my chance. I think Patricia saw something in me and thought "this is the girl".

I needed treatment and an operation in the UK. I remember swimming in England and going to the beaches. It was a great time and I did not want to go back to Uganda. Patricia helped me, and when I left everyone at Warren Farm I was crying but Patricia gave me a story album which I still keep today.

When I moved back to Uganda it took me a while to get used to it. Whenever Patricia visited she would come straight to my home. She would always enquire about me; everything was "Juliet, Juliet". She was a great friend to me. Whenever I needed anything all I needed to do was ask her. All my life has been moving with Patricia. We would have been together my whole life but she wanted me to have my Ugandan culture. I have benefitted from Patricia – she has helped me a great deal. I want to start a Patricia Foundation to thank her for her work. She inspired me – now when someone says "Juliet, help me in this", I do. I now have a house and a shop and it is all because of Patricia. Our relationship has always been very good, very strong and, even now, I still feel loved.

* * *

Kehinde Adeyemi spent a lot of time with Patricia at Warren Farm from the age of five to 15 during the 1980s and 1990s. He is currently an actor.

Warren Farm was a place where you would hear the sound of children soaking up as much of the place as opportunity would allow. This is my journey to Warren Farm. Before we take the ride along a road towards the cluster of barns and houses we spot the red letter box that we will post letters back home to the people. At the mouth of the long road to the farm is Patricia's cottage with walls as white as chalk, with geese and a pond. There was nothing disappointing about Warren Farm; totally satisfying everything a child and young teen needed.

There was the car park with parents dropping off their kids for the summer or for the year – old recruits as well as new ones. On the other side, the little apple orchard, and after that a hill that climbed and climbed and joined other hills and then went off into the horizon. This wall I would climb and balance upon as I walked all along it to a cluster of rocks and white slabs and slates of rock. As a kid it seemed like a mini mountain or cliff face, which I would always climb to the top of with my brother to marvel at the little world hidden in between the slabs – things growing and crawling. I would sometimes lift up slabs to reveal the secrets of crawling creatures, worms and shrubs.

After meeting new friends, I would go to the barn, a building made of the most ancient-looking wooden beams and banisters. Here is where the TV room was, and I remember films like The Sound of Music with its songs still swimming around inside my head. We watched Oliver Twist, Mary Poppins, the cartoon Animal Farm, a farm favourite Charlotte's Web, which is about a farm, and Chitty Chitty Bang Bang. Sometimes there would be a film or two for the older children like E.T., Star Wars or Back to the Future.

After TV in the barn, you could take refuge in the main house of Warren Farm with its beautiful dusky brown thatched roof. There was a black heavy long bar bell that rang like an ancient clock when you pulled it down beside the heavy wooden door with black iron tapered belts nailed across its top and lower parts. And then Libby, Sarah, Patricia, Sally, or many of the visiting helpers from all over the world, would let you in.

My next stop would always be the play area in the living room with this mild cream colour carpet, a white table. I would climb on to a rocking horse and rock for a long *time. Then to the library filled with books for children, where I would spend time reading. Then, it would be tea and then dinner. Your parents would stay for either or both. And here you'd have that ever familiar mix of hoping they go sooner so you can begin immersing yourself in this dream come true, before they are back again to steal the dream from you, and at the same time wanting them to stay so you can have one last hug and kiss before you see them again or they call on the phone.*

You would always seize the opportunity to see Patricia, to catch up with this awesome lady who from a child's perspective was almost overwhelming, constantly gleaming and mysterious. She would often be driving some of the kids to various activities. I always fought to be in Patricia's car on these drives; this is when I forgot how shy I was. A place in Patricia's car wasn't always guaranteed but made any trip a tranquil experience: she drove her famous station wagon like a pilot, and I always remember this feeling of serenity and safety. I would enjoy being hypnotised by passing through the English countryside, seeing other farms, wild horses as well as farm horses. On these drives, I would have time to wonder about Patricia (what does she do while in her cottage when we are asleep?), or would be carried away with childish doings. I always wanted to know everything about this wonderful woman.

Chapter VI

Bringing hope through education: The birth of Kulika Uganda

While Patricia set up her children's home at Warren Farm, in Uganda political and economic turmoil were unravelling the social fabric of the country. Amin's legacy was a bitter one. It has been estimated that his regime was responsible for 300,000 deaths and its erratic brutality fundamentally eroded Uganda's rule of law. Opposition politicians and independent journalists were targeted, including Father Clement Kiggundu, the editor of the Catholic daily newspaper, the *Munno*, who was murdered by the regime in January 1973. When Amin expelled Ugandan Asians in 1972, Uganda lost 90 per cent of its trading and commercial community, and his use of patronage to entrench political allies spread corruption throughout the public services – a blight which no later government has been able wholly to eradicate. Patricia learned of the atrocities perpetrated by Amin in letters from the now Bishop De Reeper and her many other friends in the country. One of those friends, a mother of seven, wrote on 26 March 1979, that Amin's "army men broke into our house. They fired several shots at [my husband], who was trying to escape, as men in our area had been taken by the military by force". This was a far cry from the country Patricia had left and where she had expressed "great excitement in being in on the building of a nation". In 1974 she had been able to comment to a family gathering that "a country like Uganda is still small enough that everyone has a part to play. You are not just a cog in a machine, and in a small way you feel that you can make a real contribution, and your efforts are really appreciated".

As well as the wanton brutality, Amin's regime was disastrous for the Ugandan economy. Between the early 1970s and 1981, Gross Domestic Product (GDP) fell at a rate of 2.6 per cent a year, while the population increased at an annual rate of two per cent. Exports collapsed while the price of imports increased. Spare parts for machinery became scarce, while the country's infrastructure deteriorated for lack of repair and maintenance. The decline of the economy was accompanied by a build-up of inflation, with prices rising at a rate of 40 per cent a year between 1971 and 1978.

Facing such hardship, the professional and skilled workers, upon whose labour Uganda's future depended, left in their droves. The Ministry of Education's proportion of government expenditure stayed the same and they were still able to perform the complex administrative function of national examinations without scandal and on time. Yet, the struggling system faced growing demand. Between 1969 and 1979 enrolments to primary schools rose from 600,000 to 1.2 million, requiring funds to build around an extra 230 new schools per year. Despite efforts to increase school capacity, only 56 per cent of children of primary age group were in school by 1980. Under these circumstances, Uganda's tradition of educational excellence and quality declined severely.

Yet if the dictator's fall to Tanzanian troops and Ugandan exiles in April 1979 was heralded as a victory, it was short-lived. The victorious forces permitted widespread looting that destroyed much of the remaining economy and public infrastructure. The following year was marked by a series of unstable governments, until Obote regained power in widely disputed elections in December 1980. One of the Ugandan exiled leaders, Yoweri Museveni, responded by raising a formidable guerrilla force, the National Resistance Army (NRA), establishing a liberated zone in the Buganda bush, just north of Kampala in the Luwero Triangle. Obote's counter-insurgency strategy probably resulted in more civilian deaths than occurred nationwide during the Amin regime. Obote held on by force and patronage for four and a half years, while the government committed extensive human rights violations. The war went increasingly badly for Obote up until its end, when the NRA seized Kampala in December 1985 and Obote was forced into exile in Tanzania, eventually to die in South Africa in 2005.

During all of these years, Patricia maintained a keen interest from a distance but did not visit the country. Having received her inheritance, following the death of her father, she established the Kulika Trust ('Kulika' being Luganda for 'congratulations') as a charitable foundation in 1981 and through this she was to take up the idea of providing scholarships and begin sponsoring students from the Commonwealth, among them Ugandans, some of whom had come to Britain during the civil war. It was to become one of the oldest and largest locally managed non-governmental organisations in the country, changing the lives of thousands of Ugandans.

Patricia later said:

> In Britain, very few people knew anything about Uganda other than Idi Amin and bloodshed. The only Ugandans in the country were those who had arrived as refugees. From these we were able to select a few for scholarships. During the first five years we sponsored 42 students from 11 different countries, 27 of whom were Ugandan.

In January 1986 Museveni was sworn in as the new president of a failed state. A few months prior to this, as the war was coming to a close, Patricia had decided to go to Uganda mainly to see how the Nsambya Babies Home and the children had come through the war and also to start making connections to find suitable candidates for sponsorship through scholarships in various specified subjects.

Aside from correspondence with her friends in the country, Patricia, like many in Britain, knew little of how the previous 15 years had affected ordinary Ugandans. In many ways she found that Obote's rule had exacerbated the trends of the Amin years: public facilities were crumbling; skilled and professional workers were increasingly emigrating; and the country's finest educational institutions had declined. For Patricia, this visit brought home the new realities of a country she once knew so well. She recounted:

> This visit was a real eye opener. I learnt what it meant when a country is on its knees. Kampala was badly damaged. There was nothing in the shops. Everyone was frightened and had a tale to tell, and I was a new audience. I went to Nsambya and Rubaga Hospital, which I knew well of old, and asked for applications for training of the much-needed staff in the hospitals. Of course, everyone wanted to study in England if only to get away from home.

By the 1990s, only half the country's school-age children were enrolled in school, and approximately half of those who did start school dropped out before they had mastered basic reading, writing, and arithmetic. The flight of skilled professionals had continued apace: 20 per cent of the 1980 graduates had emigrated overseas. A shadow had fallen even on Uganda's prestigious university, Makerere, which had once been the vibrant home of east Africa's literary greats, such as the famous activist playwright, Ngugi wa Thiong'o, who has been harassed by authoritarian regimes for his activism and has been tipped for a Nobel Prize. A former student, Professor David Rubadiri, the then Malawian ambassador to the UN, commented:

> When I came back [to Makerere University] in 1991… I found a group of extremely brave and daring young people. At that time, even paper to take notes was difficult to get, books had been looted, and students killed. There was murder there. It was murder of the mind, of books, of the university. But great institutions always refuse to die.

Patricia was determined to help rebuild the country through her scholarships. Her dilemma was how to choose the right candidates. Friends directed her to Basil Kiwanuka, a man who worked as the education secretary at the Catholic Secretariat on Rubaga Hill. When Patricia met Basil for the first time, he was in his late 40s: a man who had lived a full life and in whose person Ugandan hospitality combined with the organised, common sense approach of someone used to British colonial administration. During the 1950s, he had won a scholarship to study mathematics and geography at the University of London and then the University of Aberystwyth, a time which he enjoyed, aside from the occasional racism he experienced. Upon his return, Basil taught in a school before becoming the chief inspector of schools and then clerk-secretary of the East African Education Council, working with Milton Obote, Jomo Kenyatta and Julius Nyerere to 'Africanise' former colonial examinations. As Patricia put it, Basil was the man whose signature was on every 'O' and 'A' Level certificate.

He had retired from this prestigious position in 1982, and when Patricia first met him, he was fulfilling a new role, working under Bishop Ssentongo, looking to find international scholarships for Ugandan students and planning the creation of a new university. Basil recounted the occasion:

> One day, the bishop invited me into his office and sitting there was a lady. It was Patricia. We were hungry educationally, and suddenly there comes this lady. She said her ideas, and I responded: "Yes, madam. This is possible."

In Basil, Patricia had found the ideal person to set about the work of rehabilitating Uganda's massive loss of skills. She later reflected:

> Basil and I recognised that this was a marriage made in Heaven and that is how the Kulika Trust started in Uganda. We encouraged all of the scholars funded by Kulika to make suggestions about what in their experience were the biggest needs in

Uganda. This proved an excellent way for
Kulika to reach right to the grassroots.

At its core, Kulika was based upon Patricia's
determination to help rebuild Uganda. Basil was
amazed at Patricia's spirit: "She was trying to help this
country develop – educationally and in every other
way. I was happy to be a part of it." Basil began by
creating his committee, and the relatively easy task of
finding potential scholarship candidates, as "we were
full of applications". These were initially sent over to
Britain, to the Brenninkmeyer family's philanthropy
office where Brian Evans would collect them and take
them down to Warren Farm for Patricia to assess.

Once Basil had established his committee in 1986, the
massive volume of applications began to be shortlisted
in Uganda on the basis of merit, the national need of
the professional skills, the aspirations of the
individual, and his or her potential role in rebuilding
Uganda. As the years passed, the scheme expanded to
include more technical and vocational training. As
Basil mentioned, the rebuilding of Uganda needed all
sorts of skills, after all "a doctor cannot operate
without a nurse". Scholarships were also awarded for
universities and colleges within Uganda, cutting down
on the need for the expensive travel to Britain.
Throughout all this work, Brian Evans was struck by
Patricia's love of Uganda – she always wanted to do
more. As with all her activities, she attached huge
importance to establishing personal relations with
each of the Kulika scholars who were based in Britain.
Consequently, she introduced an annual Christmas

lunch in London, where all the students sponsored by the trust in Britain were invited to meet each other and the board members. For a long time this was the only opportunity for board members to meet with the young men and women whom Patricia was sponsoring. It allowed people to take back to Uganda a cultural experience they would never have otherwise had.

Yet for Brian, working with Patricia was always full of surprises. In 1988, on his first trip to Uganda, he and Patricia had an appointment in Entebbe and the only way to get there was by borrowing The Grail's Volkswagen Beetle. There had been a very heavy rainstorm so as they drove from Kampala to Entebbe they noticed that soldiers at a checkpoint were sheltering under the trees. Patricia slowly passed them but they showed no interest. However, an army sergeant came running across the road forcing the car to stop. He was unhappy that Patricia had not stopped at the last checkpoint. He did not accept the explanation that the car had slowed but the soldiers had shown no interest. Ordered out of the car, the instruction was given that the boot be opened. Neither driver nor passenger knew where the boot latch release was nor could the manual be found. By this time the sergeant and the armed soldiers, some of whom were no more than boys, who had by now joined him, were growing impatient. Brian then found the release under the glove box and opened the boot, which proved to be empty. They were allowed to continue their journey.

In the mid-1980s, the Ugandan government had very little money for higher education and institutional donors, such as the World Bank, did not view it as a priority until the 2000s. Yet throughout this period, Kulika was picking out dedicated, intelligent Ugandans, and giving them the chance to excel for their country's sake.

The value of these people to Uganda today is inestimable and of astonishing diversity. Andrew Rugasira has become one of the country's best-known entrepreneurs who founded the Good African coffee company, the first African packaging and roasting factory to export directly to the UK and British supermarket chains such as Tesco and Waitrose. Wenceslus Rama Makuza is the current head of the Ugandan Civil Aviation Authority responsible for all air traffic flying in and out of the country. Gladys Kalema is one of the world's leading veterinary experts on great apes and winner of the Whitely Conservation Award, backed by Sir David Attenborough, for her televised work protecting mountain gorillas. All these, and many others, were set on their journey to the top of the professional ladder with a scholarship from Kulika.

The lives of many people, some who have gained eminence in Uganda, have been irrevocably changed as Patricia realised her ambition to help to build the country riven by dictatorship, brutality, war and corruption. Since the beginning of the scholarship scheme, over 30 years ago, more than 1,500 Ugandans have been awarded scholarships to attend higher education institutions both in Uganda and in Britain. All of these students have been carefully selected, and have acquired certificates, diplomas, degrees and post-graduate qualifications that have been significant in their careers. Importantly, they have used their skills and qualifications to serve their country and its people.

Yet in the 1980s, as times changed, Patricia became increasingly aware that Ugandan development did not rest on professionals alone. This realisation led her attention to the development of sustainable organic agriculture in Uganda – perhaps Kulika's greatest achievement.

* * *

Bishop Henry Ssentongo is the Catholic Bishop of Moroto diocese in the North Eastern part of Uganda. He was a long-standing friend of the Brenninkmeyer family and was involved in the governance of Kulika Uganda from its inception.

Patricia is a highly gifted person but very simple and humble. Talking to her or dealing with her, one would not know that she is a big personality with a solid financial base. She has a clear vision and determination to achieve the goals she sets, with the courage of even taking risks. She has the gift of listening to people. I think this has contributed a lot to the success of Kulika.

Patricia cherishes Christian values, for example, the love of neighbour. She has special love for the disadvantaged, people with disabilities and rural poor people. Under the education programme, Kulika has a particularity which

I may call a "special charisma". This is the promotion of professionals of high calibre in different fields. There are not many organisations which have such an objective.

Patricia should be very happy and rejoice because God has blessed her work. Many beneficiaries of Kulika throughout Uganda, deep from villages, institutions, companies, banks, government ministries, hospitals, universities, etc. are prosperous, very happy and sing the praises of "mother Patricia". The big challenge they have is to embrace the spirit of Kulika and keep Kulika going for many generations to come. I see in Patricia another Blessed Teresa of Calcutta.

* * *

Peters Musoke currently practises as an advocate in Uganda's high court for Shonubi, Musoke and Co. Advocates, which has been ranked among the top brands of Chambers Global. As a newly qualified lawyer from Makerere, he was awarded a scholarship by Patricia to study international business law in Manchester. Upon returning to Uganda, he went on to root out corruption in the public sector following its entrenchment by the despotism of Amin and the counter-insurgency of Obote. He was chairman of Kulika's board of directors from May 2003 to June 2009, and in June 2010 was appointed chair of the trustees of the charity, navigating the organisation through difficult legal and human resource issues.

I had graduated with a bachelor's degree in law from Makerere in 1982 and was practising at a firm, yet longed to have the status to make a difference in the country. To achieve this, in July 1984, I was admitted into the University of Manchester to read for a Master's in international business law. My chances of taking this place, however, were close to zero as costs were debilitatingly expensive. That was when I heard of Patricia who was offering scholarships to people that wanted to rebuild Uganda. I decided to try my luck. I travelled to Nsambya with a handwritten request for a scholarship and met Basil Kiwanuka. He took me outside and, under a tall mango tree, asked what would be the purpose of a lawyer holding a Master's qualification. I responded with my vision for Uganda in which hard work for the good of society was rewarded. Patricia agreed to fund the scholarship.

Studying in England was not easy. I lived on a small stipend, while my contemporaries received grants that adequately covered their living costs. What we did in three years at undergraduate level, we did in three days in the Master's programme. The course opened my eyes to every area of law. I did not visit London until Patricia brought all the graduates together there for Christmas lunch. I never thought about staying after graduation. Uganda offered me opportunities that I wanted, and I couldn't forget about all my old friends and relatives. In 1986, I returned. In a few years I was appointed to a high-profile job as the secretary of the National Housing and Construction Corporation. This job was a good way to influence policy but was also a political minefield. I worked there for 15 years. Surviving so close to politics required tact: you needed to make a few enemies here and there but not fall for easy temptations – like the urge to steal. I worked on some of the most difficult aspects of embedded corruption that had emerged since 1972. To raise money for the war against Tanzania, Amin's government privatised significant amounts of state-owned housing. Among the many civil servants who were living in these reduced-price tenancies, a common practice emerged of selling the houses at market rates but claiming that the sale had been made at the government-fixed reduced-price rate and pocketing the difference. Amin stored the currency accumulated through these sales in Libya. This was lost forever after he fled to Saudi Arabia in 1979. Yet the loopholes remained, and it was these that I worked to close. My success in doing this made me secretary of the corporation by 31, a very young age for a post that usually went to someone in their 40s or 50s. In this job the guns come out for you.

Patricia impacted on me personally, professionally, and financially. Patricia is one of the kindest people I've ever met. She's my heroine. I've attempted to emulate her: I've become a Rotarian because of her – this is all about service and ensuring the best is given to all people. When you have become chairman of Kulika, you are very prestigious – you are known throughout the whole country and are looked to as one of the elders – ask anyone on the street! Everybody knows somebody, who knows somebody, who knows somebody that has benefitted from Kulika.

* * *

Rose Nasimiyu is a teacher at Makerere, one of Africa's historic and most prestigious universities. Rose grew up in Karamoja, North Eastern Uganda – one of country's most remote corners, a harsh land of deep red dust, plagued by seasonal drought, which Patricia visited in one of her most exciting adventures. The Karamojong are historically agro-pastoralists, cattle herders who wander during drought with their herds. In their culture, cattle play a central role and are a requirement for bride-price. Because of this, women often have a marginalised role and Karamojong clans violently raid others with fire-arms for cattle, making it one of the world's most violent regions. There is deep hostility toward outsiders, formal education and government: in 1950, the clan's elders rejected all outsiders and performed a ceremony of 'burying the pen' – the pen being a symbol of British colonialism and outside attempts to transform their way of life. In 2006, 82 per cent of the population were considered to be living in poverty. Against these odds Rose, with help from Patricia, managed to forge a career and stands as a role model in Karamoja.

I was one of those who brought problems by being a girl. My mother, by having five girls, had not done her work. My father was a tailor and my grandfather worked with Anglican missionaries and was a church teacher – he taught his children that there was nothing they could not achieve. My father sent me to the local primary school in Amudat parish run by local Catholic missionaries. I beat all of the boys in tests and examinations. I loved education and paid close attention. Yet as I approached nine years of age, social pressure began to build up. The local community, who had rejected education, referred to my educated family as "lost people", losing their culture and favouring outsiders' ideas. Yet, I was able to convince my father. I said: "I will be a highly educated, successful career woman. I'm not like other girls."

Together with assistance from relatives, my father sent me to a secondary school run by the Sacred Heart Sisters, where I was exposed to literature. I had a far-fetched idea, which was encouraged by my literature teacher Sister Wilson: this was to study for a degree. I just laughed: how will I ever get there? One day, Sister Wilson asked me if I was interested in studying for a degree, as she'd heard of a woman who gave scholarships for bright people that wanted to change Uganda. In 1985, I wrote Patricia a letter of request. A few months later, her response came. It was positive: Kulika was impressed with my commitment and would provide me with the opportunity to study literature at the University of Sussex.

Within the first week of arriving in the UK, I went to Patricia's house, where I was made to feel very much at home. Patricia is a simple, down-to-earth person brought up in an advantaged family. At Warren Farm Patricia kept goats and drank their milk, did things herself and would show people what to do and be part of it. She put herself in the shoes of those she was longing to help; she became a mother to every one of us. She enriched our experience, like a visit to Windsor Castle. She makes a difference in people's lives, not only financially, but also in ideas. Patricia's house was always full of people, and she treated no one differently from anyone else.

After four years, I went back to Karamoja and began teaching in Moroto High School in 1997. I and others have changed things in Karamoja. For instance, in 2003, there was a symbolic 'unburying the pen' ceremony when the Karamojong accepted the importance of education. People are beginning to be interested in money these days, and are interested in education, not just cows. But, within two years of teaching, a close friend of mine was shot dead on the side of the road. I considered my options, as a teaching position had opened at Makerere. I felt there is no place you can't get to, you just need to remove some of the obstacles. I applied and to my surprise I was accepted. I became a reference point in Karamoja. People were impressed and couldn't believe that I work in the university, what people call 'the city of ideas'. Patricia enabled me to achieve my dream and be a career woman. My career has helped me, and I've achieved my dream and mission to make people aware: do not undermine girls. Patricia is a great, strong visionary woman: a woman with a big heart who believes in equal opportunities for all, empowering the disadvantaged to define for themselves their future.

Chapter VII

Planting seeds and building lives: Kulika Uganda and Ka Tutandike

There are just over 4,000 miles between Warren Farm in Streatley, Berkshire, and the middle of Kampala. Travelling between one and the other, Patricia started thinking of a process that would create a somewhat unlikely link between the two.

Sitting in an aeroplane between Uganda and England during the last month of 1991, she was overwhelmed by the scale of the Sahara Desert below her. The spectacle filled her small window for almost two hours and Patricia's focus was characteristically not on the transcendent quality of the vision – it was, as ever, on people. The vast barren desert could create only one seed in Patricia's mind – a focus upon the frightening "fact that it is creeping ever southward". She ardently felt that Uganda needed to protect its land by sustainable cultivation, not least because she had witnessed, on the trip from which she was now returning, how the Ugandan civil war had drained the villages of not only the physical manpower for agricultural work but also the less tangible and more important agrarian skills that had been learned by those who had died.

Travelling through Uganda with her charity officer Brian Evans, one underlying thought punctuated everything that she saw – people were suffering in the villages. They had spoken to various families and community groups during their visit and during these conversations they received several requests for the training of farmers. Patricia's empty farm back in Streatley gave salve to her worries from a plane window: perhaps Warren Farm could provide a training centre for African farmers.

Warren Farm closed as a residential home in 1991. The climate for residential care was changing at this time, making it very difficult for Warren Farm to continue to be run in its unique and idiosyncratic manner. It was unusual in the first place for a home to be set up by an individual instead of an organisation or local authority (and, not too much later, more by private companies), rarer still that one person would be so personally involved in such a place. Patricia was involved in every aspect of the administration and in the day-to-day running of the home. She knew each and every child in the home and her involvement was vocational as much as professional. But national policy changes militated against the continuation of Warren Farm, according to Terry Connor, the former director of Cabrini Children's Society, who was at the time brought in to advise on the future of Warren Farm.

There was, says Terry Connor, a greater emphasis made by local authorities on placing children in their care in adoptive and foster homes rather than placing them in residential care. There was also the expectation that those children placed in residential care should be living as close as possible to their local communities, which ultimately meant that the rural location of Warren Farm was viewed as a drawback.

In addition to this, the model that Warren Farm was based upon – that of the family group home – was, according to Terry Connor, appropriate for younger children but the changes brought in meant that older rather than younger children were now the children for whom local authorities were seeking placements. Again, Warren Farm seemed built for a different age and the changes in policy meant that the accommodation, setting, style of care and experience of the staff were less geared towards caring for the more troubled and troublesome teenagers being referred there by local authorities.

Acknowledging that the challenges brought about by these changes could not be overcome, Patricia reluctantly closed down her group home in 1991. She had also come to realise that she was not as energetic as she once was. She was also aware of others with similar projects, who, when the time came, had run them – and themselves – into the ground rather than retire. Patricia did not want that to happen to her and her enterprise, and was wise and courageous enough to discern the situation. She put Warren Farm on the market but could not find a buyer for the property. This lack of interest eventually proved a blessing because her empty farm lying idle would soon be prospering not only as a farm but one which caused ripples, then waves 4,000 miles away in Uganda.

Patricia's idea to use Warren Farm as a training centre for farmers from Africa was greeted with energy and deep interest by those that she spoke to back in England. Her hours mulling over the idea on the plane had not been wasted and she says with typical modesty: "To my surprise all the people I talked to at home, who knew far more about African agriculture than I did, far from ridiculing the idea, were very enthusiastic about it."

Things moved quickly and efficiently. Patricia formed a small working party to help her to enact the changes she desired. This consisted of Reverend Mervyn Temple, who had cycled across Africa and been imprisoned in Zimbabwe for political reasons, Matthias Guepin, a Dutch expert in organic agriculture, Brian Evans, and herself. They had Warren Farm surveyed and the fact that it had contained a small but productive farm during its time as a children's home meant that it was deemed fit for purpose by the surveyors.

Dr Anne Stone was appointed as project manager. Fresh from a doctoral programme in agriculture at the

University of Reading, she was a proponent of sustainable agriculture with a wealth of experience in agriculture in developing countries. Patricia says that her arrival led to a great deal of action: "From then on the whole thing took on a far more professional tone." Having an expert in African agriculture in the form of Dr Stone proved invaluable. In Uganda, agriculture accounts for over half of the GDP making Patricia's decision to help in this area a wise and important one. In an article for *The Independent* in May 1998, Patricia was quoted as saying: "The best way to help the country is to increase its manpower, with medical and academic assistance."

She wanted Warren Farm to provide education that would help to improve the effectiveness of Uganda's small-scale farmers. However, this meant that Warren Farm would take a direction that was removed from Patricia's training and her initial great passion, as a social worker, for caring for children. When it was run as a children's home it was a direct continuation of her work in Uganda that she could not carry out in the country because of the civil war at the time. Apart from running a small farm, Patricia, while a keen gardener, had no actual training in farming so this all marked a distinct step away from that which was familiar.

Patricia approached this task with vigour, and she changed the farm wholesale. One of the Warren Farm trustees, John Albert, recounts Patricia's view that "you either do it or don't; it's all done or not done at all". He praises the fact that "Patricia does things properly – she's not a short-cut merchant". This proved important for organic farming because "you have to do it properly", from the most elementary materials to the overarching organic methods. Patricia's approach as "a purist" played its role in settling the ethos of the farm.

Patricia's experience with children in Uganda did, though, have a vital connecting link with farming – moving through Ugandan villages, she had no shortage of images of small-scale rural households. She recalls how the children whom she encountered from families with no money to pay for secondary school education would go off and farm themselves because they have learnt farming at school. They would do this "even at that young age, usually under the parent's wing somewhere, but they are the ones who look after the animals".

Patricia recalls with pleasure that these enterprising children are very proud of it all. Using endearing phrases like "my goats and my chickens", she says that they are useful and earn their keep. On a very small scale, she was able to see the importance of farming, at least at a subsistence level, to a normal family living in a rural Ugandan village. She realised that through training farmers she could offer more sustainable change for the good of the country as a whole. The endemic causes of rural poverty could be combated and thus poor nutrition and the lack of sustainable livelihoods could be overcome.

Her insight emerges out of the seriousness and sheer starkness of the central problem facing the people she encountered: "Families needed to grow food and get an income from the land." Four out of five Ugandans are farmers who use only traditional methods to grow crops and keep small numbers of livestock. Over 90 per cent of the farms in Uganda are smallholding farms from which the farmers make very little money. Their farms do not produce goods for the global market. They feed the farmer's family and make a small living. Subsistence farming could be developed and replicated if more effective methods were learnt. Success here could be circular – more efficient and useful farming methods could generate a surplus, which could be sold, bringing in money to be reinvested elsewhere.

What made the training at Warren Farm particularly forward looking was that it promoted training in sustainable organic agriculture. The most common small-scale rural household farms in Uganda automatically operate as organic farms in all but name. Because the farmers do not have enough money to buy expensive chemicals, insecticides and fertilisers, they must rely upon natural methods. Efficient training in sustainable organic farming thus seemed the perfect fit for Uganda. Uganda's level of organic farming stood out even among African nations where the use of artificial pesticides and fertilisers is generally very low. The lack of availability of chemical fertilisers and the lack of training in proper fertiliser use means that Ugandans add only around one kilogram of fertiliser per hectare of farmed land. This is less than three per cent of the amount used in East Africa and it is only 11 per cent of the already very low sub-Saharan African average of nine kilograms per hectare. While this meant less productivity for some quite conventional crops, it provided the opportunity to propagate sustainable organic methods.

Patricia became a passionate believer in organic farming. She saw it as the means to secure the essential food security needed for a fully functioning, healthy society. Education was situated firmly at the centre of this belief: by training skilled farmers to make them efficient producers, the social and economic circumstances of those around them could be transformed. A strong agricultural base is of paramount importance and high standards of education in the means to create this base became the focus of the work carried out at Warren Farm. Patricia was deeply concerned about the educational structure needed to train successful farmers. She wanted the Ugandans that she met to be able to use their high level of intelligence that was being overlooked because they were not given any opportunities. She wanted to help Ugandan farmers to improve their own situations, to become self-sufficient, sustainable organic farmers.

Central to this was the syllabus that was drawn up by Dr Stone in the first year of teaching. In October 1993, the first two trainees arrived at Warren Farm from Uganda – Elijah Kyamuwendo and Josephine Kizza. According to Patricia, with Dr Stone and other helpers, they turned Warren Farm into a working farm. The presence of these two vital Ugandans and the expertise of Dr Stone meant that it was made "sure that the syllabus was truly applicable to the Ugandan situation for which it was intended". This, then, was training specifically designed by an academic expert and by Ugandans with hands-on experience and detailed knowledge of the precise needs of their fellow Ugandan farmers.

Alastair Taylor, who joined Warren Farm in 1996 as a technical agricultural adviser, saw that "Patricia had a vision and she was prepared to do it". Despite the fact that she was "bringing Ugandan farmers to train in Berkshire in the cold", he saw this as "a really bold step", but felt that "bold steps, thinking ahead" were Patricia's hallmarks that led to successful ventures. And the training at Warren Farm, even during the chill of an English winter, did prove educational and extensively useful. An in-depth knowledge of specific crops and the means by which to farm organically and sustainably were still learnt.

As Andrew Jones, the man hired to head the Kulika UK Trust and board member of Warren Farm, recounts, despite it seeming "a quirky thing" and despite, too, expected questions of "what's the relevance of training an African farmer on the Berkshire Downs?", there was still the essential science behind it. This universal knowledge was still learnt and transmitted: because the education was firmly centred on fundamental principles taught through classroom sessions and then applied in the fields, it didn't matter where you did it.

Elijah Kyamuwendo recounted his first journey through Berkshire to Warren Farm in 1993, when he saw extensive gardens for the first time in his life. This green corner of England looked quite different to what he was used to in Uganda. At Warren Farm he was advised and trained how most efficiently to grow the crops, like corn, that were familiar to him from back home in Uganda. He maintains that "what was key was that we walked through all the principles and practices of sustainable development". Therefore, a far-reaching and rigorous education in sustainable organic farming was provided, each important aspect was learnt to be applied by the trainee farmers when they returned to Uganda. As chemical fertilisers and insecticides were avoided, students learnt that "you need to persuade the soil to be with you and care for you. If you mistreat it, it runs away".

Patricia maintained a central role at Warren Farm, investing time and care in overseeing the work of the trainees. Alastair Taylor recalls that Patricia was always very welcoming, helped no end by the fact that her cottage was set firmly beside the farm. She was fully involved, helping in each aspect of the farm's day-to-day running.

Whenever Rose Nasimiuyu Rotuno, who was in Britain studying on a Kulika grant, visited the farm she was made to feel very welcome. She observed that "Patricia becomes part and parcel of the help" whether this involved "digging compost or manure, or helping to make yoghurt, she would learn and then help". She would also welcome the trainees into her house, having dinner with them a few nights a week, thereby living up to her reputation as 'down to earth'. She made the visiting trainees feel completely at home at Warren Farm, which greatly improved their quality of life while training at the farm. According to Alastair Taylor, Patricia coupled her hands-on approach with an astute awareness that surrounding herself with very good advisers would lead to the greatest development for the farm. She needed experts on sustainable agriculture to get ideas, which, in turn, she built upon and learnt from.

The positioning of the training centre in England also seemed more sensible than it might at first have done when the trainees travelled to other successful farms in the country. Elijah recalled having useful and highly educational access to different farms in England at which he and his fellow trainee, Josephine, were able to meet lots of local farmers. Observing good practice and talking to farmers about their specific techniques and means for overcoming obstacles proved highly fruitful. Being in England allowed them the time to conduct these conversations and meetings. The simple fact of access to such farmers made England an ideal setting for the initial training of these first crucial trainees. Through these visits, Elijah learnt how to manage small enterprises and this help and education meant that, when he returned to Uganda, he could make use of all the skills he had acquired. After seven months training, he returned to Uganda in April 1994. He was eager to put everything that he had learnt into practice and "flew back with a lot of energy".

Back in Uganda, he immediately got to work using methods learnt from his prized English training. He used specific sustainable organic agriculture techniques, improving his methods and showing those farmers around him how to feed livestock efficiently through the land, thus completing an organic agricultural loop without the need for added unnecessary expense. He successfully transferred the skills he had acquired in being able to use manure from livestock. In so doing, he created a distinct interest and energy around his farm; it became a draw for others in his community. As a telling sign, he proudly recalls that during his first year back from Warren Farm he raised the healthiest and most beautiful cow in the village, which became an attraction.

Those around him were keen to learn the secrets of his success and the momentum from the training of one person at Warren Farm began its continual growth. Community interest in the success of others proved a useful force, in the words of Sym Kiwanuka, a former chief executive officer of Kulika: "If you can grow a good banana, people want to know the secret of your success."

Patricia visited Elijah in Uganda to see what they had achieved. She showed the intense personal interest that was the hallmark of her time helping children. Her urge to see the individuals that she helped, to see that they were well and prospering, continued through her work in agricultural training. Elijah said that for him it was a moving time, to have worked in

Britain and then to see Patricia in his village and compound revelling in the fantastic work that he was carrying out. For him, Patricia was "a human being with a very big heart" shown by "the care, the concern, the love she offered poor Ugandan farmers [which] was spectacular. I will never ever forget it."

When Dr Anne Stone left Warren Farm in 1997, Dr Ian Wallace of the department of agriculture at the University of Reading was contacted. He was an African agricultural expert and fellow proponent of the need for sustainable organic agricultural methods, so he seemed the ideal person for the work being carried out at Warren Farm. He and Dr Rachel Percy of the university's agricultural extension and rural development department became consultants to Warren Farm, working very closely with the team at the farm.

A link was also set up with the university in 1997 which allowed the trainees at Warren Farm to be registered as students of the university to take a Post-Experience Diploma in Sustainable Agriculture and Farmer to Farmer Extension (SAFFE). These qualifications lent the whole project at Warren Farm much academic credibility, building on a recognised body of knowledge and creating a team of well-trained organic farmers who were academically and institutionally recognised.

The farmer-to-farmer extension training meant that the central aim of Warren Farm's progression – to be run by Africans for Africans – could be carried out because the trainee farmers could spread and transfer their new skills in sustainable organic agriculture from Warren Farm to Uganda. The initial trainee farmers became key farmer trainers themselves once they finished at the farm and the university. This meant that the students were not solely chosen for their commitment to learning about sustainable organic agriculture, but also for their ability to communicate effectively with their fellow farming Ugandans so that the knowledge and skills that they had learnt could be most efficiently passed on to others.

In 1999 the initial Warren Farm trainees flew back from Uganda to Warren Farm to take part in a special training session. This would equip them to spread the skills learnt at Warren Farm to those in Uganda, and to bring the farm's education in sustainable organic agriculture back to their fellow farming countrymen. Elijah Kyamuwendo was a vital part of this contingent and during the same year he received an MA degree in agriculture from the department of agricultural sciences of Imperial College London. Again, education and academic recognition helped further the cause of those trained at Warren Farm.

Between 1993 and 1999, 40 students graduated from the course and even those who had not taken part in the special training session naturally helped to spread the message of sustainable organic agriculture to the other farmers in their communities. They spread their skills learnt at Warren Farm through local organisations and other farmers in the community, through women's groups and marketing organisations. Small-scale rural farms were transformed into profitable businesses, their success founded upon the principles of organic farming. One student recalled at the time that "the land is the blackboard for my farmers". Education came through practical application leading to the cherished 'green ground' that spoke to its success. Another student, Joy Okech Nsubuga, returned to grow coffee for export, bringing economic success that was not dreamt of during her initial days spent as a subsistence farmer. Perhaps more important, Joy set up a demonstration garden on her farm in Uganda, which helped local growers to learn how to share in her success by emulating the techniques that she learnt in Berkshire.

Thanks to their training, those taught at Warren Farm steered clear of what Patricia feared: the "modern farming methods [that] damage the ecological balance and ultimately create economic dependency". Patricia's idea was working really well, cemented as it was by the academic credentials bestowed by the University of Reading. The university also introduced the training model to Makerere University in Uganda thanks to a formal link between the two institutions. This relationship was helped by British Council funding in Kampala through the British Council's higher education links. This further spread the training that originated at Warren Farm which finally emerged, according to Alastair Taylor, as "really different from other organisations, something to challenge usual ideas".

The reach of Warren Farm and Kulika was extensive: the former chief executive, Sym Kiwanuka, states that "in every place, we have someone". As Rose Nasimiuyu Rotuno says, all the people that Patricia helped, in turn helped the nation and "her vision has worked out". Rose sees the work of everyone helped by Warren Farm and Kulika as an extension of Patricia's vision, founded upon a belief in making a difference in whatever you do. This notion of a self-sustaining legacy is repeated by Father Sekalega, headmaster of St. John's Secondary School in Nandere, Uganda, who says that within each of the teachers, lawyers or doctors helped by Kulika scholarships and the farmers who have been trained, there is a strong acknowledgement in the worth of "having benefitted yourself, ensuring that you help somebody else". Patricia says: "What a great achievement for all who took part in it."

Patricia still talks modestly about Warren Farm, according to Madeleine Lustigman, who had previously worked for the Red Cross, and worked closely with Patricia as a project and programme manager and a funding adviser, from 2006 until 2013. When urged to explain how the farm was set up, Patricia would rarely elaborate. But she "was at her happiest when charitable work took up her whole life" and would often talk about it informally. She loved farming, recounts Madeleine, and, during trips to Uganda, she seemed to take the most enjoyment from visiting 'Kulika' farms. She would bring seeds from England to give to Ugandan farmers and relished most of all seeing training put into practice and producing tangible results.

Patricia's enjoyment is also confirmed by Jane Leek, director of Porticus UK, when she says of Patricia: "Put her into Uganda – she fits". The wealth of people benefitting from Patricia's work in Uganda formed a community within which she felt most comfortable. Rose Nasimiuyu Rotuno calls it a family that continues her work.

The decision to move the agricultural farmer training programme to Uganda and the consequent closure of Warren Farm marked the beginning of a new chapter for Kulika, first set up in 1981. Running the new programme was going to require the significant revamping of the *ad hoc* administration. Since 1992, Basil Kiwanuka had handed over much of his responsibilities in administering Kulika to Sym Kiwanuka. Sym was exceptionally bright and had written a new computer science course for the Examinations Council during the Amin regime before completing his PhD in physics and teaching at Temple University in Philadelphia in the USA. In his time, Kulika Uganda comprised a few administrators in the spare office of Nsyambya Babies Home, where Patricia had worked in the 1970s.

The lack of infrastructure was obvious. For most of the 1990s, the Ugandan team's only means of communication with Britain was through the office fax machine of one of Sym's lawyer friends or a pay phone at the central post office. To manage the complexities of the agricultural training, Kulika began to expand, employing Elijah Kyamuwendo as the co-ordinator for the new community development programme, assisted by a few other key farmer trainers with Alistair Taylor as a technical adviser.

This small expert team faced a giant task. Their aim was not to transplant Warren Farm from the Berkshire countryside to the tropical soils of Uganda, but to improve the livelihoods and wellbeing of rural communities across the whole country though sustainable organic agriculture. Alistair Taylor points out: "Patricia's focus on organic agriculture was ahead of the time in the late 1990s. It was not as common then as it is nowadays. In Uganda, of course, it fitted perfectly." There was a dire need for these skills, as basic knowledge had slowly ebbed away through decades of civil war, government mismanagement of education, and the HIV/AIDs epidemic which between 1990 and 1998 affected betwcen 12 to 16 per cenl of the adult population. As Elijah commented:

> In Uganda we have two types of erosion. Firstly, soil erosion, eroding the soil down into the valleys. And secondly we have the erosion of knowledge, skills and attitudes. The erosion of the soil is a result of the erosion of skills. Many of these skills we have lost in the wars and because of disease. People have died along with their knowledge.

He argued that rural communities could be revived through the proper use of land. The community development programme that they designed, therefore, did not simply train farmers in agricultural techniques but in a broad range of skills and practical understanding of healthy diets, the importance of hygiene, basic financial accounting, managing savings, and selling to markets. Elijah recalled:

> The first market is the kitchen: you must be able to feed yourself and the family. The second is the local market to feed those around you and to generate money for school fees and hospital bills. Finally, we sell to the third market, the export market, and make money which we can invest in the country.

For some in Uganda, peace was not realised with the end of the civil war in 1986. In 1987 in Soroti, in the east of the country, a woman known as Alice Auma Lakwena launched the short-lived millenarian Holy Spirit Movement against the government. This foreshadowed the much more tragic rise of Joseph Kony's Lord's Resistance Army (LRA) which, in 1991, began a localised resistance to the Museveni government in Acholiland, in the north of the country, killing and terrorising civilians and abducting children for use as child soldiers. It has been estimated that 30,000 people have been abducted by the LRA since then.

Elsewhere, outside these violent corners of the country, the mood in the late 1990s was very different. Many Ugandans were beginning to feel optimism about their future. President Museveni was implementing a progressive agenda of democratic rights and the rule of law, decentralisation, and encouraging interventions from international non-governmental organisations to address some of the country's social problems, such as health and education. A *New York Times* article in 1997 stated that he had "started an ideological movement that is reshaping much of Africa, spelling the end of the corrupt, strong-man governments that characterized the cold-war era". This optimism of the late 1990s was shared by Kulika in developing its community development programme.

The Ugandan programme began with discussions between the Ugandan team and Patricia, Andrew Jones, and the Reading academics that had set up the farmer-to-farmer extension training at Warren Farm. Andrew Jones, who had worked with agricultural centres in Kenya, and Patricia were wary about recreating a Warren Farm in which money and time were wasted on building a centre rather than 'getting the message out'. He explained: "So, we established a rolling programme... the principle being that you didn't establish a centre." By taking the Warren Farm programme and training one local community over a few years and then moving to another community, Patricia and Andrew sought to create a programme that helped the Ugandan communities that needed it most. With this decided, Elijah and Alistair began their first centre in Masaka – a district ideal for the growing of coffee and bananas – 87 miles southwest of Kampala, on the western shores of Lake Victoria.

Taking over the Masaka District Farming Institute, the Kulika team rehabilitated their water supply and took in their first intake of key farmer trainers in 2000. As with all Kulika training, each trainee had to agree to pass on the skills they acquired to up to 30 other farmers, the theory being that once these skills are in the local networks they spread by themselves. Just like at Warren Farm, the first intake were taught how to farm using only things which came from the land beneath their feet. Using no pesticides or artificial fertilisers, the practical training covered the basics of organic farming: how to stop soil erosion through building terraces, how to plant trees and dig ditches, how to make natural pesticides, how to plant tea to encourage crop growth, how to mulch to prevent weeds, and how to retain water.

Through the course many widely held misconceptions were also addressed, especially around diet and vegetables – particularly among men – who were shown how much they could reduce their medical bills through having a more balanced diet. By simply building sack mounds – a sack of soil for growing – or kitchen gardens, farmers could cheaply use a small plot of land to provide all the vegetables they need.

Money, too, was a key area of training. Elijah, a keen amateur inventor, taught farmers how to use a fuel-saving stove which produced less smoke, used 60 per cent less fuel, and which was safer for children than the three stone hearth traditionally used in Ugandan homes. Trainers were taught how cash crops, such as shea nuts and coffee, could be grown to bring in income, while Kulika teams taught farmers how to plant, prune, stump, pulp, ferment, and dry premium coffee. By growing coffee bushes and banana trees on the same area of land, farmers could use less land and grow more and better quality crops. Among the many other areas addressed by the training, farmers were also encouraged to leave some land untouched, rather than chopping trees and creating fields, for natural habitats to survive. Bill Bruty, an adviser to Kulika, wrote in a report for the organisation:

> John, a farmer, had arrived in the village with nothing, apart from a barren plot of land strewn with boulders. With basic hand held tools, he had dug a drainage trench which captured the torrential rain waters and defined the perimeters of his territory. With the same tools he had steadily removed every boulder. Rocks were replaced by a small matoke [savoury banana] plantation, and cassava was interwoven with beans and coffee. There were occasional mangoes and even an orange tree.
>
> His compacted, cast-iron land was lifted up and fed with water, manure and compost.

Four years later, his family now have a
varied, nutritious diet and the coffee brings
enough cash for his three children to go to
school.

He says: "The land was not the first.
Hygiene was the first. Without hygiene
you have no health and you cannot work
the land. When I finish in the fields I clean
my hands. My tools are stored away from
my bedroom. My floors are clean – there
are no jiggers. Hygiene is the first... Others
don't change their ways because of my
wisdom. They don't change because they
see my farm. They change because my
children are at school and they want that,
too."

Throughout the first five years of the community
development programme, it had moved from Masaka
to the more arid district of Tororo on the eastern
border with Kenya, then up to the neighbouring
district of Pallisa, before moving to the west of the
country towards the great central African mountain
range of the Ruwenzoris.

The model, with its link to the University of Reading,
worked so well that the country's Makerere University
took it as an example for its agricultural models. As
the farmer training began in earnest, Sym, Andrew
Jones and Patricia were creating new partnerships as
part of the educational scholarships programme. In
1999, Kulika began working with the Open University

to offer a distance-learning MSc course for the country's non-profit development professionals. To date, this course has trained over 85 leading Ugandan professionals in civil society and non-profit organisations. Dr Gordon Wilson, director of the development and international studies department at the Open University, praised the exceptional quality and experience of the students. These partnerships have been of great value to the non-governmental sector in Uganda.

The movement of operations to Uganda led Patricia to confront herself about the future: she still had much of her inheritance and was determined, according to one charity adviser, to give all her money away. She believed deeply that Ugandans should be trusted to shape their own future. So, together with Andrew and Sym, Patricia resolved on setting up Kulika Uganda as a fully Ugandan-run organisation, entirely separate from Britain, with an endowment from her funds.

In 2001, Patricia, Andrew Jones, and her brother Thomas, as well as the new Ugandan team, decided the plan for establishing an independent Kulika Uganda by 2006 at a conference in the picturesque town of Jinja, which sits on the shores of Lake Victoria and claims to be the source of the river Nile. Andrew Jones orchestrated the countdown to the independence of Kulika Uganda and the consequent closure of Kulika UK, which was a mammoth undertaking.

Andrew, Sym and Elijah established a board of Ugandan professionals, which included a bishop and notables such as Patricia's old friend Elizabeth Namaganda, now in charge of The Grail on Rubaga Hill, where Patricia and Elizabeth used to live in the 1970s. Andrew recruited a young accountant, Joseph Kasibante, and trained the staff in all aspects of professional administration.

The establishment of an independent Kulika Uganda in a country still mired with the widespread practice of corruption had the beneficial effect of allowing other organisations, such as a schools link programme called Food for Thought, to work with Kulika safe in the knowledge of its accountability. In 2002, Andrew secured a National Lottery funding grant, held by the Kulika UK Trust, for £100,000 due, in part, to Kulika Uganda's new accountable financial systems and reporting. Yet, as Andrew recollects, Patricia found that difficult, as she was always slightly uncomfortable with the professionalism of the organisation. She regarded it as her money and it was an inconvenience being governed by trustees.

Despite these tensions, Kulika Uganda continued to grow. In 2003, Sym retired and into the new position of chief executive stepped Kulika's head of community development, Elijah Kyamuwendo. From a humble background in Mubende, a district just west of Kampala, Elijah had distinguished himself though his intellect and charismatic leadership at Warren Farm, and in setting up the community development programme with Alistair Taylor. His humble charm and moral leadership had endeared him to the Kulika board and Patricia. He was father to two boys of his own and 18 adopted children – many of whom were orphaned by the blight of HIV/AIDS. Explaining why he took them in, Elijah said:

> The reason I am keeping these children, educating them and giving them a life is that I believe in the proper growth of children, I believe in childhood values, and I also believe that I am contributing to the reduction of children who live on the streets.

After one incident in which one of his adopted children ran away, Elijah found the boy sleeping rough and convinced him to return. He remembered: "It took me a year to bring him back to normal life. But now he has finished his course to become a vet and he is leaving my house to make space for a younger man."

From 2003, when he was appointed chief executive, to 2012, when he tragically died of cancer, Elijah helped Kulika Uganda to grow into one of Uganda's largest Ugandan-run non-governmental organisations employing 41 staff and with funding relationships with new donors such as the EU, Uganda Telecom, Coca-Cola, the Royal Society for the Protection of Birds (RSPB), Concern and the Bank of Africa. Over these years, Kulika set up new projects across the country, including an organic coffee certification scheme with the EU; a forest conservation project with the RSPB in the mountainous Echuya Forest bordering Rwanda; and women's empowerment training among poor communities in the arid terrain of Nakasongola in the centre of the country.

Patricia did not always agree with the direction in which Elijah took the organisation – most notably in 2007 when he stopped the rolling training and bought 41.5 acres of land in Lutisi, a village outside Kampala, to set up a permanent training centre. Yet she stuck to her belief that Uganda's future lay in Ugandan hands and supported Elijah in his times of need. In 2008, she reiterated her belief in "the far-sighted, confident way the charity is being managed today; Kulika's future is in safe hands". Sue Errington, one of Kulika's trustees, has pointed out that central to Elijah's success was his being "the practical person as well as the intellectual". As Elijah explained:

> I never gave up farming. So even now I set time aside over the weekends and holidays to farm and feed my family. I go home every weekend, get the tools out and do my work in the garden. It helps me to keep leading by example.

Indeed, such was Elijah's pride in farming that prior to one of his visits to Britain he had his visa application turned down when he had written that he was both a farmer and a chief executive on his application form. The British visa administrator had taken it as a joke. The mistake was amended and the British High Commissioner personally gave Elijah back his passport with his visa included.

Patricia's great fondness for Elijah was, in part, because he was such an excellent ambassador, a man who was living proof that Kulika's community development programme worked. Yet as, Sue Errington described, it was only because of Patricia that Elijah was able to achieve what he did: "Elijah was such an intellect, but that could only be realised because Kulika gave him that opportunity." And it was not just Elijah who had been given the chance to determine the course of his life. By 2012, Kulika Uganda had trained over 10,000 key farmer trainers, improving communities in nearly every district in Uganda, which had an immeasurable value among their local communities.

By the mid-2000s, with activities in Uganda continuing in their own right, Patricia and Andrew Jones began to consider the future and whether there were completely new directions to take. Andrew was convinced Patricia should establish a community development foundation for East Africa, but her heart belonged to Uganda and particularly to its children. Because of this, Andrew conducted two research projects into the situation of deaf children and the levels of literacy among young people in Uganda.

Yet, cracks inevitably began to appear in their relationship. Despite Patricia's charitable motives to spend her money helping Ugandans, she became frustrated that charities the size of those she had established need the infrastructure – the accountants, the organisational strategies, and the due diligence – which caused her so much irritation. This and the lack of clear roles between Patricia and Andrew, still chief executive, meant their working relationship began to unravel. Andrew eventually left after the Kulika UK office closed in 2005. He remembered Patricia as being "awkward, confrontational but with her heart in the right place". Patricia a few years later commented that Kulika has a lot "to be grateful to Andrew for."

Patricia decided the remainder of her money should be split two ways: half would support Kulika and the remainder would be used to set up a new charity to help disadvantaged Ugandan children. All Patricia knew at this stage was that the new organisation would work in three areas: children with disabilities; encouraging children to read; and child care for the disadvantaged.

Patricia didn't want to be specific about how Ugandans themselves should determine matters but she did have her predetermined thoughts on each of the areas. The new organisation was named Ka Tutandike, Luganda words for "let's get started". On their first trip together to Uganda, Patricia and Madeleine Lustigman, building on Andrew Jones' reports, visited leading professionals and academics specialising in deaf children and early childhood literacy. Madeleine recounted: "They looked at us like we were mad… and basically said go away, get some priority areas, get a strategy and come back."

Despite Ka Tutandike's name, it quickly became apparent that working in Uganda in 2006 was much more formal than it had been with Basil in the 1980s.

The tensions that Patricia had felt with the professionalisation of Kulika arose again: she wanted something to happen, and just get started. But there was so much process she wasn't used to. Through a painstaking amount of research and administration by Madeleine, Patricia was able to hire Christine Semambo Sempebwa as Ugandan chief executive in 2007. She was a charismatic civil society leader and a former teacher, who learnt sign-language when the organisation began working with the deaf.

Working together Patricia, Christine and Madeleine got started. In addressing child care for young disadvantaged urban children, their research had pointed out the dire situation surrounding market sellers' children. Across Kampala's slum markets, to keep children out of danger and to stop them trampling on other market sellers' produce, mothers would make them sit near them, either in a merchandise box or among their produce. According to the *Ka Tutandike – Let's Get Things Started!* newsletter in 2010, this caused all sorts of problems for the child:

> Unable to play or make friends, children are instead surrounded by often aggressive and vulgar behaviour, which can seriously damage the child's emotional and mental development. Mothers, too, find it difficult to cope with child care at work, particularly as they lose trade because customers see children as dirty and unhealthy.

Because of the complex set of problems for parents and children in the market, Ka Tutandike commissioned a study in 2008 of the situation in three markets in Kampala. The study mapped out what welfare provision already existed and identified ways in which Ka Tutandike could help to improve the lives of market children. This study resulted in Ka Tutandike establishing an early years project, which worked with a hundred babies, toddlers and children and 50 parents to increase the quality of early childhood care in urban markets.

One story to emerge out of this programme was that of a baby girl called Tendo. For hours she would be left among heaps of charcoal with dust slowly caking her face. By the time she was eight months old the situation was dire: Tendo was severely malnourished, weighing only 3.5kg and deathly ill. As Tendo's mother recollected: "She developed measles until her tongue became black." But little could be done. Medical treatment was too expensive for her mother and would have required spending hours and sometime days away from the market queuing to be seen. Maama Tendo, however, had heard of a small day care centre, funded by Ka Tutandike, called Miles2Smiles, which had just opened up outside the market and was offering secure and affordable care. She decided to take Tendo. Seeing that death was certain if nothing was done, Catherine Kitongo, the owner of Miles2Smiles, agreed to take Tendo on and began feeding her a daily meal of mukene, a silvery fish that is rich in protein, and soya flour. Tendo's condition improved. The result was that Tendo became a healthy, confident child who enjoyed telling stories and has many friends to play with. Maama Tendo, freed from the simultaneous challenges of child care and work, attended the centre regularly and became one of the most active mothers there.

The second area that was close to Patricia's heart was reading for pleasure. As Andrew Jones' report had highlighted for her, the under-investment in education and limited teacher training opportunities meant Ugandan primary school students were very likely to be illiterate. It was not just at school that children were turned off reading. Juliet Nalukwago, a primary 5 teacher at Kasubi Church of Uganda Primary School, said: "More reading should happen outside the classroom, with children reading at home with encouragement from their parents". Juliet said that books were expensive and what books were used were those already at the school.

The Ugandan education system became desperately overstretched after the introduction of Universal Primary Education (Education for All) in 1997. Many young pupils in Uganda were taught in huge classes, some with as many as 200 students, with few teaching materials, and perhaps one book to share between five. Low paid and often untrained teachers struggled under a strict education curriculum focused on examination success. Ka Tutandike, therefore, began a programme of simple, local changes which encouraged reading stories for pleasure.

Under Patricia's direction, Ka Tutandike commissioned an internal research report into reading for pleasure in Ugandan primary schools. Through interviews with three head teachers, nine school teachers, 22 parents, and 54 pupils, the government department responsible for literacy and various other organisations involved in promoting reading, the charity established a reading for pleasure project. The project consisted of a simple training scheme in cataloguing and highlighting good practice to allow children to access library books, as well as setting up 'reading tents' in three Ugandan schools: St. Paul Banda Primary, Ttula Primary, and Kasubi Church of Uganda Primary.

Patricia's last area of focus was about people living with disabilities. Following the same pattern Madeleine, Christine and the team did their research on where there was most need. After consulting with 120 people, Ka Tutandike found that the area of need in the deaf community which was least served was the need for sexual and reproductive education. Responding to this, the team built a project which sought to improve access to reproductive information for 500 disabled children in Masaka. They interviewed deaf children, their parents and community leaders, teachers of the deaf as well as nurses and health advisers. Ka Tutandike began working in partnership with the Ugandan National Association for the Deaf (UNAD), run by deaf people for deaf people, and Naguru Teenage Information and Health Centre, experts in reproductive health. In a Ka Tutandike report, Nassozi Kiyaga, founder of Deaf Link Uganda, said:

> Deaf people in Uganda are excluded from all kinds of information and are not valued as human beings. From birth, the family becomes an immediate aggressor by rejecting the child and treating him/her as a burden and misfortune. Due to lack of communication deaf children miss out on the socialisation process. Being deprived of acquiring a full language, deaf people are isolated, cut off from ordinary sources of information readily available to the hearing populations, such as radio, TV, public announcements, and so on. They have little or no access to education as preference and priority is given to hearing children. Knowledge of reproductive health among deaf youth is abysmal – almost non-existent. If it is present, it is always misinformed and shrouded in myths – which they obtain from other deaf people. There is a belief that deaf people do not need reproductive health information, that they are asexual and do not have sexual emotions. Due to the communication barrier their needs are not understood.

Therefore, with Patricia's blessing, Ka Tutandike, acknowledging the right of deaf people to reproductive health information, in collaboration with the deaf community, sought the best ways in which teachers could provide the information to deaf children. Ka Tutandike trained health workers and parents and community members in sign language to give deaf children access to health services and to change negative attitudes towards deaf children. Even though she was largely based in England, Patricia's role was not simply to provide financial support. Madeleine explained: "Patricia lit the fire within these people... her involvement infiltrated right down to the bottom of the projects."

Yet, as the organisation developed, Patricia was becoming aware of her own age and acutely concerned that Ka Tutandike needed to be self-sustaining after her endowment had ceased. With this in mind, she asked Heidi Kruitwagen to join the organisation as a trustee in 2008. Heidi was a member of her extended family with a background in corporate finance with UBS. Her appointment marked the beginning of a sea change in the Ka Tutandike's direction, as Patricia stepped back from the directional activities of the organisation.

New technology was now having a bigger impact on communications through its increasing visibility, availability and status in Uganda, and helped to establish relationships with government and other non-governmental organisations working on disabilities. Within the following two years, Ka Tutandike had set up the Ugandan National Coalition for the Deaf, a collective of civil society organisations working on deaf issues. In the spring of 2010 Ka Tutandike hired Anisha Rajapakse as an experienced development professional who had worked for over 15 years in international development and for the Commonwealth. In 2010 Patricia decided to hand over the chair of Ka Tutandike to Heidi.

Under this new leadership, Ka Tutandike developed their programmes and narrowed their focus to achieve a more sustainable organisation. They focused, for instance, on groups such as the Umojja Women's Group, which was founded by three women market vendors from the Nakawa market led by Mudemuki Shamila, a charismatic Muslim woman, trained as a midwife and a boxer! This collective of 76 female market sellers, sought to work together to end the stigma and discrimination faced by women living with HIV/AIDS by training them in core entrepreneurial skills. Ka Tutandike supported them in training in organic agriculture; the provision of referral services at the local health centre; and the provision of child care at nearby day care centres for some of the 300–500 young children that spent their days at the market. The group also sought to expand their jewellery and crafts businesses. Both Heidi and Anisha helped them create new and fashionable designs which significantly boosted their sales. As a result of their increased earnings the women bought a paper-cutting machine, which enabled them to increase significantly their income from their jewellery sales.

This reorientation towards social enterprise meant changing the organisation. Both Heidi and Anisha, worried that these changes might sit uneasily with Patricia, were amazed when, during a trustee meeting,

Patricia having listened intently, gave the response: "Well hurry up and do it!" Anisha saw this as an example of the practical nature of Patricia's approach: "[She] was very ahead of her time in her thinking about development and the need for people to be self-reliant. The concept of social enterprise and promoting self-reliance – that's what she always wanted".

Eventually the Ugandan board hired a new chief executive, Susan Kisitu. As a social worker she had worked for 23 years for the Ugandan Society for Disabled Children, initially as a field worker in Luwero supporting children with amputations and polio, and finally as its chief executive. Susan is a farmer and keen entrepreneur, yet her approach to children mirrored Patricia's when she was at CWAS: "The basic responsibility of looking after the children lies with the family."

Heidi saw this development of Ka Tutandike as a lot of minds working together, "weaving a pattern". She was convinced that Ka Tutandike needed an element of self-sustainability, and so, committed to leading such change Heidi, at her own expense, took a course in social enterprise at INSEAD, the world-renowned Business School in Fontainebleau, outside Paris.

Even since 2011 Patricia's charity has evolved from being a traditional one, dependent on donors, to what it is today. Its move toward being a social enterprise has meant that it is working to become self-sustaining, while empowering its beneficiaries economically so that they become self-reliant and break free of donor dependency. This is exactly what Patricia wanted in terms of her legacy for Uganda. When her funding ended, she wanted the beneficiaries ultimately to take charge of making their lives better, using their own skills and initiatives.

The journey from 2011 to 2013 did not prove to be an easy one. Tough decisions had to be made regarding issues of performance, accountability and impact on the ground with the Ugandan operations and management. After an organisational review, an HR audit and staff assessments, the old team have gone. Today a new team is led by a dynamic chief executive and a committed chair and board of governors who have taken charge of ensuring that Ka Tutandike will be sustainable in the future.

The UK trust has attracted a new and prominent group of professionals as trustees, able to provide strategic advice and guidance, when needed. Patricia was proud of the calibre of individuals attracted to her charity, in Britain and in Uganda. She was even more delighted in knowing that they had a similar passion and commitment that she exhibited many years ago to ensure that the poor and vulnerable are empowered to have a better life and provide a safe and secure future for their children.

In enhancing their status, the team began developing strong links with influential Ugandans, including Alex Ndeezi, Uganda's first deaf MP. Together with the Commonwealth Secretariat and Leonard Cheshire International, Ka Tutandike led the organisation of the first national symposium on education of the deaf and hard-of-hearing child in Uganda in August 2011 in a hotel on the outskirts of Kampala. The aim of the symposium was to identify best ways to educate deaf and hard-of-hearing children in Uganda, and determine the roles of different institutions in addressing the needs and aspirations of deaf people, developing a common approach among the organisations.

The recommendations of the symposium were subsequently taken up by the Ugandan government and they agreed with Ka Tutandike's request for the Uganda Coalition of organisations working on deafness to contribute to the next special needs education policy for Uganda. Ka Tutandike had become an important resource for developing the government's national strategy for people living with disabilities.

In attendance at the symposium were luminaries from the political world and NGOs from all over Uganda, all brought together at the instigation of Ka Tutandike. Remarkably, however, 85 per cent of the other speakers during the conference were themselves deaf.

Patricia and her brother Paul had travelled to Kampala to attend this event, and were duly shown to their seats of honour in the front row. As they waited for the proceedings to begin, they started to muse over the potential and the momentous success of the day and then somehow, they let their minds wander more widely, reliving the winding path of Patricia's working life in Uganda and England. Then Paul said: "You must be proud of all you have achieved". She rather avoided the answer by expressing her gratitude to those hundreds of committed people who have worked so hard and long to bring about this phenomenon. Paul pressed her again about how she really felt. She thought for a moment, and turning to him, she replied, "Well I suppose I had the ideas".

* * *

Sym Kiwanuka studied at Temple University in Philadelphia where he also taught as part of his MA. He worked on particle physics but he felt that this would not apply back in Uganda, and could not pursue it there. He returned to Uganda for the 'good jobs' that he had heard about from friends during the time of Idi Amin. He taught in various secondary schools and then moved on to work for the East African Examinations Council. He eventually became the executive secretary of Kulika.

Patricia bought me books on astronomy and science. I was able to visit Patrick Moore [the astronomer] and went to use his telescopes at his home. All of these things came through Patricia; she was a great help.

Most important, she had a lot of love for Africa. She was a rich person who never showed she was rich – from her dresses, her house in the UK to her cars. In Uganda, she was pious, always attending mass. She stayed in the poorest of places. She stayed with The Grail and she cooked and ate poor matoke. She visited poor areas and ate her students' food, always saying "Don't prepare special stuff" wherever she went. She gave out money only when it was an important cause. She advised her people: don't throw money on anything with sympathy, be strategic with your donations and help. Small random donations will not help. There are ways that we can help even more.

* * *

Canon Sentongo is an Anglican priest who lives in Kampala and was brought on to the first board of Kulika Uganda. He assisted on the education scholarships committee.

Here was a lady who really had a mind for others, a heart for others. I have no hesitation in looking at what this lady achieved in the years that I was associated with Kulika, in the results that were achieved throughout Uganda, through the women and children's programmes that were launched. If Uganda has a Mother Teresa, this must be the one we have. Patricia came here and lived here for some time before she established Kulika. She's an unpublicised Mother Teresa for Uganda. She's done so much and still does.

Bibliography

Biggs, Vivien (1978), 'Private fostering' in *West African Families in Britain: A Meeting of Two Cultures* (edited by June Ellis). Routledge and Kegan Paul

Ellis, June (editor) (1978) *West African Families in Britain: A Meeting of Two Cultures.* Routledge and Kegan Paul

Janoff, Sandra (2010), *A Thriving Karamoja: Creating Possibilities Together.* Unicef Uganda

Kasozi, AB, (1994), *The Social Origins of Violence in Uganda: 1964–85.* McGill-Queen's University Press

Matthysen, Ken, Finaldi, Sergio, Johnson-Thomas, Brian, and Danssaert, Peter (2010), *The Karamoja Cluster of East Africa: Arms Transfers and the Repercussions on Communal Security Perceptions.* International Peace Information Service

Mbiti, John, S (1989), *African Religions and Philosophy.* Heinemann

Odaet, C (1990), *Implementing Educational Policies in Uganda.* World Bank Discussion Papers

Philpot, Terry (2001), *A Very Private Practice: An Investigation into Private Fostering.* British Agencies for Adoption and Fostering

Rhodes Paige, John (2000), *Preserving Order Through Chaos: The Survival of Schools in Uganda, 1971–1986.* Berghahn